NOTHING MORE AND NOTHING LESS

NOTHING MORE AND NOTHING LESS

A Lent course based on the film
I, Daniel Blake

VIRGINIA MOFFATT

DARTON · LONGMAN + TODD

First published in Great Britain in 2017 by
Darton, Longman and Todd Ltd
1 Spencer Court
140–142 Wandsworth High Street
London SW18 4JJ

ISBN 978-0-232-53344-6

A catalogue record for this book is available from the British Library

Produced and designed by Judy Linard.
Printed and bound in Great Britain by Bell & Bain, Glasgow

This book is dedicated to the memory of
Karen Sherlock
and all victims of benefit cuts.

A message from Paul Laverty, screenplay writer of *I, Daniel Blake*, for readers of *Nothing More and Nothing Less*:

'Good luck with this Lenten project and I hope it leads to some lively debate, and action. I hope people from all sorts of backgrounds, religious and none, can use the film *I, Daniel Blake* to see how power operates in our lives. I think the systematic abuse by the State, especially by use of companies like Maximus – a sub-contracted American company, who gets so many decisions wrong (some 60 per cent of appeals against them are successful) – assessing our most vulnerable, raises profound moral and political questions.'

CONTENT

INTRODUCTION

A TIME FOR REPENTANCE

'Repent and believe in the Gospel' are the words spoken to us on Ash Wednesday as our foreheads are marked in ash. As we hear them we recall the beginning of Jesus' ministry, when, just after John the Baptist's arrest, he invites people to join him:

> 'The time is fulfilled, and the kingdom of God is close at hand. Repent and believe in the gospel.'
>
> Mark 1:15

Like Advent, Lent is a season of preparation. But while the former is a time of hope, as we await the coming of God's son who will transform the world, Lent is more sorrowful. It is a season when we reflect on our sins and repent of them. By imitating Jesus' forty days in the desert, we undertake acts of denial as we try and focus on our desire to change ourselves. This is an excellent way to approach Lent. And even if many of us, myself included, fail to fulfil the promises we make on Ash Wednesday, our attempts to do so help us approach Holy Week with a sense of renewed faith.

But if we concentrate just on our personal failings,

we can miss a wider dimension. For Jesus says these words just after being baptised by John, who himself has been inspired by the scriptural injunction to 'prepare a way for the Lord' in the desert, 'to make his paths straight'. John also says that 'the kingdom of God is at hand' indicating that the mission is to bring this kingdom into being in the here and now. Building the kingdom of God is not simply about asking ourselves to reflect on our individual weaknesses and strive to be better human beings. It is not just about our personal salvation, but the salvation of the whole world in fulfilment of the words of prophets like Micah:

> 'but they shall sit every man under his vine and under his fig tree, and no one shall make them afraid, for the mouth of the Lord of hosts has spoken'
>
> Micah 4:4

> 'And what does the Lord require of you But to do justice, to love kindness, And to walk humbly with your God?'
>
> Micah 6:8

In other words Jesus came to this world to ask us to repent not just of our individual sin, but the structural sins of the society that we are living in. To strive for justice, to build a world where all are equal and all live in peace. And so Lent challenges us to not just reflect on our own failings, but also the failings of our governments and institutions. It is a time when we can ask why some in our society are suffering, and why oppression happens. It is a time to question the causes of injustice and think about what we can do in response. And it's a risky business because sometimes those institutions would prefer not to be challenged, as John the Baptist and Jesus both knew to their cost.

This course approaches Lent from the broader perspective. Taking the film, *I, Daniel Blake*, we will reflect on these issues over the next five weeks. And while the film deals with a pressing contemporary injustice – the work capability assessment – it also highlights universal concerns about oppression and suffering. As the course progresses, we'll be thinking about why such things happen, how we are implicated and what we can do about it in order to build the kingdom of God.

I, DANIEL BLAKE, A STORY FOR OUR TIMES

I have been campaigning on welfare issues since 2011, so when I heard that the film director, Ken Loach, was coming out of retirement to make a film about the failures of welfare policy in the UK, I was delighted. I am a big Loach fan, and I knew that the movie would raise awareness of the problems faced by benefit recipients in the UK. The subsequent film, *I, Daniel Blake*, written by Paul Laverty and directed by Loach tells the story of one man's struggle to survive a cruel and inhumane benefits system. Just as I had hoped it has made quite an impact. It has left audiences reeling, won several awards (including a BAFTA, and the Palme d'Or at the 2016 Cannes film festival) and created a backlash from a couple of reviewers who, having never experienced the benefits system, found it hard to believe Daniel Blake's story was not exaggerated. Something the producer was quick to refute.[1]

I have always believed stories have the power to jolt us out into action and had myself been stirred into activism by a true story very similar to that told in *I, Daniel Blake*. In 2011, I read about David Groves, a former miner from Derbyshire who had been signed off work since 2008 following a heart attack and strokes. Like the fictional Daniel Blake, David was asked to undergo a work capability assessment. Like Blake, he failed, despite being too ill to work. He won his case on appeal, only to be called back for a further reassessment. And just like Blake, he died of a heart attack the night before he was due to attend; his family blamed his death on the stress induced by his experiences.[2]

Back in 2011, very few people seemed aware that this injustice was being perpetrated on sick and disabled people, except those affected, their families and campaign groups. But, as the work capability assessment was rolled out nationwide, and the 2012 Welfare Reform Act came into force, bringing with it other problems such as benefit caps, housing benefit changes and sanctions, more people have become involved. The most vocal campaigners have tended to be those most affected, particularly the disabled campaign groups, Disabled People Against the Cuts (DPAC), Black Triangle, Pat's Petition and the WOW Petition. But as awareness has grown, many others have joined suit, including Christian leaders and organisations. In 2014, vicar Dr Keith Hebden (now Director of the Urban Theology Unit), minister Simon Cross and Catholic Worker Scott Albrecht fasted through Lent to raise awareness of food poverty in Britain.[3] At the same time 40 Anglican Bishops signed a letter in protest[4] and Cardinal Vincent Nichols, the Catholic Archbishop of England and Wales, gave a powerful interview to the *Daily Telegraph*, labelling welfare cuts 'a disgrace'.[5] In 2015, the Joint Public Issues Team produced an important report on benefit sanctions, while Ekklesia and the Centre for Welfare Reform[6] published a letter from leading Catholics to Iain Duncan Smith (and later his successor, Stephen Crabb) challenging their approach to welfare.[7]

By 2016, even the politicians who instigated the changes were beginning to rethink. After a backbench rebellion on further benefit cuts resulted in a 'U' turn, Iain Duncan Smith, the former Secretary of State for Work and Pensions, resigned, suggesting that he had resisted Treasury demands for cuts. A few months later, during a meeting with me and researcher Stef Benstead, he also admitted that the work capability assessment had failed, putting his faith in universal credit instead.[8]

When Loach's film was launched at the 2016 Cannes Film Stage it helped amplify these concerns, bringing them to the international stage. This in turn has heartened activists, with many taking up the slogan, 'we are all Daniel Blake' to inspire their campaigning. We can hope that future historians will note the role the movie played in changing the narrative on welfare benefits and will stand as a testament to the cruelty of our times. But it can also have a deeper meaning for us, because, as I noted above, the film touches on some universal themes, which make it a powerful focus for Lent.

SCOPE OF THIS COURSE

This course is intended for group discussion. You may be an existing group, or you may have decided to come together to follow this specific programme. While the format suggests the group has a Leader each week, it doesn't have to be the same person each time, and sessions can be split with one person leading on the discussion and another on the worship.

The course will make most sense if everyone involved watches the film first. You might wish, as a group, to meet before Lent and watch the film together. Or you might wish to watch individually. It would be helpful if each participant thinks about what the story has shown them and asks the following questions:

- Do you sympathise with the main characters?
- Were you shocked to discover the benefits system is like this?
- As a person of faith, how do you want to respond?
- What is our Christian duty to our brothers and sisters who are in trouble?

- Why should Christians care about oppression?
- What does God ask of us?

The course will look at these questions in more depth over the five weeks of Lent that lead up to Holy Week. However, the film will also provide a springboard for discussions about other issues of cruelty and abuse.

Structure of sessions

Each session takes its format in part from three elements of the pastoral cycle: *think, pray, act*.

Think: Each week begins with a couple of clips from the film to prompt thought and discussion facilitated by the group leader. This should take about an hour.

Pray: This will be followed by a time for prayer, based on the week's theme. As noted above this could be led by the same person who led the discussion or another member of the group. This should take about twenty minutes.

Act: The session will conclude with some thoughts about further actions you could take. This should take about ten minutes.

All the times suggested are indicative. Your group can take as much and as little time as you want.

Each session has an introduction setting out some of the issues to be discussed, and a conclusion for further reflection. The group can decide to read these in advance or add them to the content of the session.

Weekly Themes

Week 1 – Systems of Oppression: The theme of the first week will be systems of oppression. Taking the work capability assessment as a starting point, it will explore what makes this system so oppressive, how it compares with other oppressive systems at different times in history, and the role people of faith can play in resisting it.

Week 2 – Staying Human: One of the striking aspects of the story is how both Daniel and Katie work hard to maintain their dignity, their sense of humour, their sense of self. This session will ask how it is possible to maintain one's humanity and dignity when living in a situation where you are constantly belittled and dehumanised. Does faith help or hinder this?

Week 3 – Compassion in the Darkness: Despite the horrors they encounter, both Daniel and Katie experience moments of kindness. Taking the Parable of the Good Samaritan as our inspiration, the third week concentrates on how compassion can alleviate suffering, and our responsibilities as Christians to not pass by on the other side.

Week 4 – Fighting Back or Giving In?: The fourth week looks at how people respond in different ways to an ongoing situation of hardship. While Daniel chooses to make an act of resistance, Katie seems to give in. The session will consider whether their actions make sense, ask us to reflect on what we might do in such circumstances and where God might be.

Week 5 – The Suffering Servant: Both Daniel and Katie suffer enormously throughout the film, enduring humiliation, poverty, lack of control. This final session reflects on the image of the suffering servant provided in Isaiah 52:13–53. It considers how Daniel's statement that he is 'a citizen, nothing more, nothing less' reflects a universal right that is denied people too often. In the light of our Lenten journey to Jesus' death and resurrection this statement challenges us to resist oppression, offer compassion, and act in solidarity with those who suffer. For this, in the end, is what Jesus is inviting us to do.

PUBLISHER'S NOTE: *Nothing More and Nothing Less* is being published at the same time as another DLT Lent resource, *Feast or Famine?: How the Gospel challenges austerity*, which explores issues of economic austerity versus plenty in a biblical context, produced in association with Ekklesia. The two courses may be studied alongside each other by individuals or groups if readers wish to reflect on these themes in greater depth.

NOTES FOR INTRODUCTION

1. '*I, Daniel Blake* producer responds to Toby Young, Iain Duncan Smith criticism', Alex Dudok de Wit, i-news, 28th October 2016. https://inews.co.uk/essentials/news/i-daniel-blake-far-scathing-says-producer/

2. 'Stress of Tory benefits killed our dad, family claims', *Daily Mirror*, 22nd May 2011. http://www.mirror.co.uk/news/uk-news/stress-of-tory-benefits-tests-killed-129934

3. 'Reverend Dr Keith Hebden to fast for 40 days and nights in solidarity with hungry Britons using foodbanks', Felicity Morse, *Independent*, 26th February 2014. http://www.independent.co.uk/news/reverend-dr-keith-hebden-to-fast-for-40-days-and-nights-in-solidarity-with-hungry-britons-using-9154318.html

4. 'Hunger is a "national crisis", religious leaders tell Cameron', Patrick Butler, *Guardian*, February 2014. https://www.theguardian.com/society/2014/apr/16/million-people-britain-food-banks-religious-leaders-faith-groups

5. 'New Cardinal Vincent Nichols: welfare cuts "frankly, a disgrace" ', John Bingham, *Daily Telegraph*, 14th February 2014. http://www.telegraph.co.uk/news/religion/10639015/New-Cardinal-Vincent-Nichols-welfare-cuts-frankly-a-disgrace.html

6. 'Time to rethink benefit sanctions', Joint Public Issues Team. http://www.jointpublicissues.org.uk/wp-content/uploads/rethink-sanctions-report-0315.pdf

7. 'Leading Catholics write to Iain Duncan Smith to express fears over benefit cuts', Damien Gayle, *Guardian*, 3rd July 2015. https://www.theguardian.com/politics/2015/

jul/03/leading-catholics-write-to-iain-duncan-smith-to-express-fears-over-welfare-cuts

8. 'The day we met Iain Duncan Smith', Virginia Moffatt, Ekklesia, 9th November 2016. http://www.ekklesia.co.uk/node/23552

NOTHING MORE
AND
NOTHING LESS

week 1
SYSTEMS OF OPPRESSION

TO START YOU THINKING

Throughout the Bible Jesus tells stories about what the kingdom of heaven is like. Matthew, chapter 25, for example, begins with the parables of the foolish bridesmaids and the men with the talents. Although the latter is open to interpretation,[1] one reading of both is that Jesus is suggesting that the kingdom of God is only achieved by the actions we take in the here and now. This seems to be confirmed by the passage that follows:

> When the Son of Man comes in his glory, escorted by all the angels, then he will take his seat on his throne of glory. All nations will be assembled before him and he will separate people one from another as the shepherd separates sheep from goats. He will place the sheep on his right hand and the goats on his left.
>
> Then the King will say to those on his right hand, 'Come, you whom my Father has blessed, take as your heritage the kingdom prepared for

you since the foundation of the world. For I was hungry and you gave me food, I was thirsty and you gave me drink, I was a stranger and you made me welcome, lacking clothes and you clothed me, sick and you visited me, in prison and you came to see me.' Then the upright will say to him in reply, 'Lord, when did we see you hungry and feed you, or thirsty and give you drink? When did we see you a stranger and make you welcome, lacking clothes and clothe you? When did we find you sick or in prison and go to see you?' And the King will answer, 'In truth I tell you, in so far as you did this to one of the least of these brothers of mine, you did it to me.'

Matthew 25:31–46

It is clear from this passage that Jesus is asking us to take care of each other – to look after the sick, hungry, poor and dispossessed. And if we think of just one of these aspects, being sick, we can understand why. However, healthy we are, most of us will have had an experience of being very ill at one time or other in our lives. It might have been a severe bout of measles as a child, a very bad case of the flu, an attack of appendicitis that led to surgery. In such circumstances, we will have been confined to bed, often in pain, and left debilitated after the worst had passed. We probably needed a reasonable amount of time to recover, and in some instances, this might have been weeks or months.

Sickness doesn't trouble most of us in our day-today lives, and once we have recovered, we rarely think of it again. But if we take a moment to look back and remember what helped us get through such a difficult time, most of us will realise that we relied on a number of vital factors. First, we had someone – a parent, partner, sibling, friend – who took care of us. They comforted us in our pain, made sure we ate, drank, took our medicine, had baths and went to the toilet. Without them, our lives would have been very miserable indeed. Second, we had somewhere safe to recuperate, a warm comfortable bed, and a roof over our head ensuring we got better as fast as we could. Finally, we had financial security, as children, our parents had the resources to cover the bills, as adults, we had paid sick leave from work.

For most of us, such periods are rare and pass quickly, but there are some people for whom illness is part of daily life. Those who live with chronic disease, such as Crohns (which affects the digestive system), Multiple Sclerosis (the nervous system), or Ehlers-Danlos Syndrome (the skeletal system), have periods of good health and poor health. When they are well, they are able to take part in most everyday activities, perhaps with some adjustments to ensure they stay healthy. When they are sick they may be bedridden for weeks, need hospitalisation, or surgery, before returning to better health. Other people may become sick from cancer, heart disease or another life changing illness. Some may become ill for a while, get better and continue their life as before, but some will never recover, either because the condition is terminal or it is permanent, having a life-long impact on health. While some disabled people live with disabilities that mean they live with frequent pain and exhaustion. All of which means some sick and disabled people require support if they are to participate in society as equal citizens. The Bible couldn't be clearer about the importance of helping sick people. Job is a righteous man, but when Satan makes him ill, many of his friends believe he must be being punished for his sins. He goes through immense pain and hardship until God comes to his aid. The story of Job shows that ill health can come to anyone. God's message here is that Job's friends should not have condemned him but should have alleviated his suffering. This message is repeated often in the New Testament when we see Jesus choosing to sit with sick people. He treats them all with compassion, even pariahs like lepers, frequently defying the Sabbath to heal people. While the Parable of the Good Samaritan, which we will discuss in Week Three, indicates how we should respond when someone is hurt.

What then is our Christian responsibility for those who are sick or disabled today? I would suggest that we have a duty to follow Jesus' example, to welcome sick and disabled people into our lives, to be inclusive, offer support to those who need help and stand alongside those who are fighting the injustice of benefit cuts. If we find this hard to do, we might want to reflect on our own past experiences of illness to remind us why we should assist people living with ill health or disability.

We would all want to be sure that people who are sick or disabled have support workers or family to dress their wounds, care for their physical needs, comfort them in pain; that they will have a secure home and a comfortable bed in which to recuperate; and that they will not have to worry about money while they are unable to earn for themselves or their families.

Sadly, this is not the reality for many sick and disabled people in Britain today. They and recipients of other benefits are part of a system that is causing immense harm, as we shall see in our first session.

Session 1

THINK

Introducing the film

We are starting by looking at two sections of the film which demonstrate the plight that Daniel and Katie find themselves in.

Clip 1, Opening credits and Scene 1/2, 1–8 minutes (till the end of Daniel's conversation with the DWP)

In the opening credits we hear Daniel's voice during his meeting with the healthcare professional at the Department for Work and Pensions (DWP). As the interview progresses, and the interviewer asks questions such as whether he can put a hat on his head, but not about his heart condition, we sense Daniel's increasing frustration. This is followed by snapshots of Daniel's life, walking through his community, visiting his doctor, seeing a friend, carving wood, till he receives a letter telling him he is fit for work. When he rings the DWP he waits over an hour, he is told he can't appeal until the decision maker rings him, and this should have happened before he received his letter.

DISCUSSION
(10 minutes)

- What does this scene tell you about Daniel as a person?
- Contrast the behaviour of the 'healthcare professional' and the doctor? What purpose do their questions serve? Do they help or hinder Daniel?
- What does this scene tell you about the DWP?

Clip 2, Scene 3, 1–10 minutes (till Katie and Daniel get kicked out of the job centre)

In this second scene Daniel arrives at the job centre to find out what he needs to do next. He is told he is eligible for Job Seeker's Allowance but if he wants to appeal he has to do it online even though he has no access to a computer. He feels a bit dizzy and a member of staff invites him to sit down where he overhears Katie getting into an argument with another member of staff.

DISCUSSION
(10 minutes)

- What do you think of Daniel and Katie's behaviour in the scene? Why do they behave like this?
- Why do the staff at the DWP behave in the way they do?
- What are the implications of staff actions for Katie and Daniel?

Thinking about both scenes.

- How did you feel about the way Daniel and Katie are treated?
- As a person of faith, what do you think you should do in response?

BROADER DISCUSSION
(20 minutes)

In this broader discussion we will reflect on the experience of other oppressive systems in history. Some examples are given below:

Russia 1938-1940: In Stalin's Russia between 1938 and 1940, labour rules were tightened to the detriment of workers. This included punishment for of 2-4 month's labour for a worker who quit a job, while being twenty minutes late meant a 25 per cent pay cut and the employee being put on six month's probation.[2]

Pinochet's Chile 1973-1990: In 1973, General Pinochet mounted a successful coup against the left-wing President Allende. Following the coup, opposition groups were rounded up and many were tortured and killed. During the worst years of the Pinochet regime, dissent was ruthlessly suppressed and left wing activists, church members and unionists were regularly tortured or murdered.[3]

North Korea present day: In North Korea today, all workers are expected to prepare for the day by reading through political instructions and end it by evaluating the day including self-criticism and colleague criticism.[4] Meanwhile, the government runs a brutal system of labour camps for 200,000 prisoners, and has a three generational punishment policy, so grandchildren can be forced to endure the punishment of their grandparents.[5]

- Can you see any links between these examples of repression and the DWP system that affects Daniel and Katie?
- Have you ever been complicit in oppression, e.g. not supporting a bullied colleague, buying goods from a repressive regime? What stopped you from speaking up? Would you do it differently next time?
- What do oppressive systems have in common?
- What should Christians do in the face of oppression?

PRAY
(20 minutes)

Reading: Isaiah 1:15–17

When you lift your hands to pray, I will not look at you, for your hands are covered in blood. Wash yourselves clean. Stop all this evil that I see you doing. Yes, stop doing evil, and learn to do right. See that justice is done – help those who are oppressed, give orphans their rights and defend widows.

Litany of mercy

Leader: For the times we have chosen to ignore political decisions that lead to oppression –

All: Oh God, we are sorry.

Leader: For the times we have failed to support a victim of oppression –

All: Oh God, we are sorry.

Leader: For the times we have been complicit in oppression –

All: Oh God, we are sorry.

Leader: We ask for your forgiveness God –

All: And commit ourselves to see justice being done.

Amen

Spontaneous prayers

Leader: We know you are God of justice and mercy. We bring our concerns before you.

(Time for everyone to pray their concerns.)

Reading: Matthew 5:1–13

And seeing the multitudes, he went up on a mountain, and when he was seated his disciples came to him. Then he opened his mouth and taught them, saying:

'Blessed are the poor in spirit,
For theirs is the kingdom of heaven.
Blessed are those who mourn,
For they shall be comforted.
Blessed are the meek,
For they shall inherit the earth.
Blessed are those who hunger and thirst for righteousness,
For they shall be filled.
Blessed are the merciful,
For they shall obtain mercy.
Blessed are the pure in heart,
For they shall see God.
Blessed are the peacemakers,
For they shall be called sons of God.
Blessed are those who are persecuted for righteousness' sake,
For theirs is the kingdom of heaven.

Blessed are you when they revile and persecute you, and say all kinds of evil against you falsely for my sake. Rejoice and be exceedingly glad, for great is your reward in heaven, for so they persecuted the prophets who were before you.'

Leader: The Beatitudes are often considered to be Jesus' manifesto for Christian living. We hear him both exhort us to act for justice, but to remember that when we are treated unjustly, Jesus is beside us. How do these words affect us as Christians?

(Short period of reflection from the Group)

Leader:
(10 minutes)
Let us all join together in the closing prayer.

Closing Prayer

God, you have given all peoples one common origin.
It is your will that they be gathered together
as one family in yourself.
Fill the hearts of mankind with the fire of your love
and with the desire to ensure justice for all.
By sharing the good things you give us,
may we secure an equality for all
our brothers and sisters throughout the world.
May there be an end to division, strife and war.
May there be a dawning of a truly human society
built on love and peace.
We ask this in the name of Jesus, our Lord.
Amen

Reprinted with permission of Catholic Online,
www.catholic.org

The final part of the session will be to think what actions people can take in response to the issues thrown up by the discussion.

ACT
(10 minutes)

The film raises a number of concerns. Decide as a group what action you would like to take in response. Here are some ideas to get you started:

- Write to your local MP asking them to support calls to abandon the Work Capability Assessment.
- Support the work of a campaign group working on welfare issues (see the resources list at the end).
- Organise a vigil at your local job centre/Maximus WCA centre.
- Find out all you can about basic income, an alternative to the current welfare system, and consider being part of the campaign for change.

FURTHER REFLECTION

In his excellent book, *Walk to Jerusalem: In search of peace*[6],the late Gerard W. Hughes SJ tells of many encounters with individuals on his journey. During one such discussion, Hughes is asked an important question. The questioner recognises Hughes' efforts, but the problems of war are so complex, he asks 'What can we little people do?'

This is a helpful question to ask when faced with a problem such as the oppressive welfare system. What can we little people do to help the real Daniels and Katies who are suffering in this way?

The first thing we can do is understand how we got here.

When the work capability assessment was first trialled in 2008 by the Labour government, very few people (including myself) were aware that this was happening. It was only those who had to undergo the assessment, and their families and friends who knew about it. Although, they raised their voices in protest, their concerns were ignored. In 2011, the pilot projects came to an end, and the then Coalition government decided to roll it out nationwide, convinced it would help reduce the growing welfare bill.

But how did such a cruel system develop in the first place? And why did politicians in the three largest political parties Labour, Conservatives, and Liberal Democrats (before the 2015 election) all support it initially? And why did Christian politicians, in particular Iain Duncan Smith, do so much to promote it?

To understand this we need to understand a number of different issues:

Models of disability
Political thinking about sickness and ill health has been dominated by different models of disability:

- The **medical model** of disability sees disability and illness in purely medical terms and these are generally negative. This model confines the individual into the role of passive patient, at the mercy of professionals who will 'fix' their problem. Traditionally, this model of disability has been promoted by the medical profession, focusing on a condition rather than a person. Or it has been used by charities who raise funds to help the 'victims' of such conditions.
- The **social model** of disability sees disability and illness as being the result of impairments that can be overcome if society is willing to make adjustments. This model of disability has been developed from disabled people themselves. It places value on the individual, as a citizen and whose life needs to be seen holistically, rather than as simply a limiting condition.
- The **biopsychosocial** model of disability sees disability and ill health as being part of a complex interaction of biological, psychological and social issues. This model suggests that the problems created by illness and disability can be overcome if people are supported to understand the roots of their illness better.

The medical model of disability was the dominant model for much of the twentieth century. This often led to sick and disabled people being at best, institutionalised, and at worst, treated dismissively by the professionals they encountered. The failure of medical institutions and the emerging disability rights movement in the 1970s brought this model to the forefront, and the social model began to take prominence from the 1980s onwards. While in recent times, campaigns by sick people have led to the idea of the 'expert' patient, who knows as much or more than the medic treating their condition, and whose views should be equal when discussing treatment plans.

In the last twenty years, the biopsychosocial model has grown in significance, as we have begun to understand that the causes of ill health are complex. It has been particularly promoted by insurance companies keen to avoid expensive claims for health related absence from work.

The rising costs of care and support

One of the positive elements of the twentieth and twenty-first centuries has been the development of medical treatments, which have resulted in people with disabilities and long term health conditions surviving longer, and older people living longer. This has resulted in a demographic problem for governments. As the population ages, there are more people needing care, and that support will often be more costly.

Governments of all political hues have been grappling with this over the last thirty years, and it is this context in which sickness and disability benefits have come under scrutiny. As the welfare bill has increased, politicians have been forced to consider whether there is enough to meet every need. A model that suggests some illness could be psychosomatic, or be improved by working, enables politicians to consider a solution other than universal benefits for those who are ill.

Faith in the market

The political consensus since the 1980s has been that the private sector generally does things better than the public sector. This led to successive governments looking to the market to help deal with the demographic changes of sickness and disability. Given that the insurance sector has been actively promoting the biopsychosocial model, it is no wonder that this model should become attractive to political leaders.

The combination of these three things, the rise of the biopsychosocial model, the growing number of people needing support and the belief that the market knows best, laid the ground work for the development of the work capability assessment (WCA).

A misguided belief, that because in *some* situations, working helps sick people stay positive, and gives disabled people meaning in their life, means that *all* sick and disabled people should, led to the development of the new system of benefit assessment in 2008. Furthermore, the impact of the bankers' crash and the subsequent austerity cuts led to a drive to cut costs, which resulted in the programme being expanded before its impacts had been properly analysed. Similar assumptions have been made about 'work shy' benefits claimants which have led to the system of sanctions from which Katie suffers.

And yet the warning signs were there from the start – initial reviews by Professor Harrington urged caution, while sick and disabled people themselves indicated this was a system that did more harm than good. However, politicians of all persuasions failed to heed the warnings until it was too late and the WCA continues to be a critical part of the welfare system. And continues to do so much damage that the UN have recently declared in combination with other cuts, it has created a 'human catastrophe'[7]

So what can we little people do?

The first thing we can do is to stand alongside sick and disabled people, challenging the government in the ways outlined in this session. But we can also go further. By understanding the roots of this system we can begin to build arguments to defeat it. And if we want to find ideas about what we could do to replace the system, there are many fine organisations who are leading the way. These include Disabled People against the Cuts, Black Triangle, the Disability News Service Centre for Welfare Reform, Church Action on Poverty, Tax Payers on Poverty, Joint Public Issues Team, Ekklesia. Details of all these organisations are listed at the end of this book.

NOTES FOR WEEK 1

1. *The Upside Down Bible*, Symon Hill, London: Darton, Longman and Todd, 2016.

2. 'Stalinist laws to tighten "Labor discipline" 1938–1940' Hugo. S. Cunningham, 1999. http://www.cyberussr.com/rus/labor-discip.html

3. 'Military dictatorship of Chile 1973–1990', Wikipedia. https://en.wikipedia.org/wiki/Military_dictatorship_of_Chile_(1973%E2%80%9390)

4. 'A day in the life of Pyongyang – how North Korea's capital goes to work', Paul French, 2nd May 2014, *Guardian*. https://www.theguardian.com/world/2014/may/02/north-korea-a-day-in-the-life-pyongyang

5. '10 brutal North Korean secrets' Andrew Handley, Listverse, 26 August 2013. http://listverse.com/2013/08/26/10-brutal-north-korean-secrets/

6. *Walk to Jerusalem: In Search of Peace*, Gerry W. Hughes, London: Darton, Longman and Todd, 1991.

7. *Government cuts have caused 'human catastrophe' for disabled, UN committee says* Ben Kentish, *Independent*, 24th August 2017.

week 2

STAYING HUMAN

Note for leader: This next section includes references to women's experience of rape; please be sensitive in preparing for this.

TO START YOU THINKING

Time and again in the Bible we find people who are struggling under oppressive systems. Jeremiah is imprisoned and constantly ridiculed for his beliefs, Daniel faces the lion's den, Samson is arrested, while John the Baptist, Jesus and many of the apostles suffer prison, hardship and death. When faced with cruelty and a system that wishes to break you, it can become difficult to maintain one's sense of dignity and self, to stay human in the face of inhumanity.

The prophet Jeremiah endures many difficulties, taking his strength from Yahweh, who makes this promise:

> As far as these people are concerned, I shall make you a fortified wall of bronze.
> They will fight against you

but will not overcome you,
because I am with you
to save you and rescue you.

Jeremiah 15:20

It is this 'fortified wall of bronze' that keeps Jeremiah going through ridicule, imprisonment and threats of death, giving him a powerful sense of hope and the possibility of change.

Look the days are coming, Yaweh declares, when the City will be rebuilt for Yahweh, from the Tower of Hananel to the Corner Gate. Then once again the measuring line will stretch straight from the Hill of Gareb, turning then to Goah. And the whole valley, with its corpses and ashes, and all the ground beside the ravine of the Kidron as far as the corner of the Horse Gate, eastwards, will be consecrated to Yahweh. It will never be destroyed or demolished again.

Jeremiah 31:38–40

Samson is famously shorn of his long hair, the source of his strength. Yet, in prison, his hair grows back, and so when he is being paraded before the people, he is able to bring the pillars down on himself and his enemies. While this story can be taken literally, it could equally be considered a metaphor for how individuals maintain their sense of self when treated harshly, enabling them to resist the system right to the end.

And, of course, Jesus, throughout his arrest, trial and crucifixion, also remains true to who he is. In the Garden of Gethsemane, he rebukes Peter for taking out his sword, and takes the time to heal the soldier Peter hurts. On the cross, he ministers to the good thief, and despite his pain, offers comfort to his mother and his disciple, John.

Such biblical stories can inspire us and help us hope that we too might manage to do this if faced with such difficult circumstances. But we can also draw lessons from fiction and real life stories. As I am writing this Lent guide, Channel 4 has begun showing a new version of Margaret Atwood's famous novel, *The Handmaid's Tale*. The book, for those who haven't read it, deals with a futuristic theocratic society where fertility rates have dropped. Fertile women are forced into sexual slavery where they act as 'handmaids' to the barren wives of the society's leaders.

Offred is in the most hideous of situations. She is paired everyday with another handmaiden, allegedly for support, but actually so they can spy on each other. The system forces her to be complicit in hatred and violence to others, because speaking out against it will result in her death. She has lost her husband, her child, her name. She has no possessions, and nowhere to go. She is regularly forced to undergo a ritualistic ceremony of institutionalised rape, where the leader's wife, sits behind her holding her hands, while she lies on the bed and the leader penetrates her.

Yet Offred is intent on survival. Her desperation

to be reunited with her daughter keeps her alive. In a moving moment in the first episode, we see how her memory of watching jellyfish in an aquarium helps her remain connected to her child, and gives her a positive image to counteract the despair of her day to day life.

Thankfully, Offred is a fictional character. However Margaret Atwood has pointed out that when she created her imaginary country Gilead, she was careful to ensure that every detail was drawn from real human societies past and present. So that, at the time it was published in 1985, many saw modern day parallels. Today's TV version mirrors the suffering of women under the Taliban, in Saudi Arabia, the Yazidi women kidnapped by IS (Daesh), and so the question is a very real one. When living in an oppressive situation that takes away every aspect of your autonomy, is it possible to maintain one's humanity and dignity?

For some, it is the passion for justice, knowing that what is being done to you is wrong, that drives a person forward. This was the experience of Yazidi activist Nadia Murad who was captured by Daesh when she was 19, saw family members murdered and was regularly raped and abused. Fortunately she escaped and fled to Germany where she now campaigns for the rights of women. As she said in an interview in the New York Times in 2016:

'Daesh took my family, my future, my life. But what I have in my heart, what I've always had is justice. Justice was on my side, not their side, and they couldn't take that from me. Despite everything they did, they couldn't take the knowledge I had that I was right and they were wrong. This will remain with me. All of the women and girls who are in their hands have justice on their side.'[1]

Another survivor of kidnapping and rape, Camilla Carr, was captured with her boyfriend Jon James, in Chechnya in 1997. When one of her captors repeatedly raped her, Carr decided that: 'the only way I could get through this horror was by thinking to myself, 'You can never touch the essence of me – my body is only part of who I am.'[2]

The rapes stopped when she contracted herpes and was able to tell her rapist, no. After he understood that she didn't want to be raped, they were able to share information about each other's lives, and though she could not forgive the rapes, she understood how traumatic his life had been and how it had resulted in him taking part in the kidnaps.

While for Norman Kember, captured in Iraq in 2006, telling jokes, praying, drawing pictures of cathedrals from memory were all ways he could maintain his sense of self in captivity.[3]

Fortunately, most of us will never experience oppression and suffering on this scale. But it is worth taking the time to think if faced with a system intent on grinding us down, how might we best respond?

Session 2

THINK

In this session, we'll take this thought about how to live humanly in an oppressive situation and see how Daniel and Katie survive the difficulties they are living with.

Clip 1, Scene 4, 1–5 minutes (till Katie gets off the phone)

This scene follows on from the one we looked at in the previous session. After they are kicked out of the job centre, Daniel helps Katie home with the shopping. The scene opens with Daniel fixing the cistern, while Katie rings her mum in London. After she gets off the phone Daniel asks her why she moved to Newcastle. She explains that she has been living in a hostel for two years with her children, Daisy and Dylan, and the council could only offer her a flat if she moved out of London.

DISCUSSION
(10 minutes)

- What does this scene tell us about Daniel and Katie?

- Both of them have much to be pessimistic about. What do you think is keeping them positive?

- What do you make of Daniel's generosity at the end of the scene?

Clip 2, Scene 5/6, 1–10 minutes (till China has helped Daniel)

Daniel attempts to fill out his Job Seeker's Allowance (JSA) form at the library but is defeated, because it takes so long to work out how to use the computer that he runs out of time. When he goes to the job centre, someone helps him but she is told off by her manager. Later he hangs out with his friends who are having a Skype call with Stan Li who has been supplying them with cheap trainers to sell. After the Skype call, Daniel's friend China helps him with his JSA form.

DISCUSSION
(10 minutes)

- How do Daniel's friendships help him survive?
- What other things do we see Daniel do through the film that help him stay true to himself?
- Daniel's friend thinks the system is deliberately designed to frustrate him. Do you agree? What do you think of Daniel's response?

Thinking about both scenes:

- Have you ever experienced a situation that seemed hopeless? How did you get through it?

- Did your faith help? If so, how?

BROADER DISCUSSION
(25 minutes)

Imagine that you are living in an authoritarian regime, where small breaches of the rules result in punishment. One day you commit a minor infringement of the law for which you receive a hefty fine and a warning. There are mitigating circumstances, so you protest, your fine is doubled and now you are marked as a troublemaker. You work for a government body and they are notified. A few weeks later you are told about a new initiative to save money. When you point out the flaws in the programme you are demoted and your salary reduced, putting pressure on the family budget. You are warned that if you raise any further issues you may lose your job. You have seen this happen to people many times, so you know it is not an idle threat.

- How do you think you would cope in such a situation? What would your main concerns be?
- What would you do to stay positive?
- Do you think Bible stories would help?
- Would faith make it better or worse?

PRAY
(20 minutes)

Reading: Psalm 31:1–5

> I come to you Lord for protection
> Never let me be defeated.

You are a righteous God;
Save me I pray!
Hear me! Save me now!
Be my refuge to protect me,
My defence to save me.
You are my refuge and defence;
Guide me and lead me as you
 have promised.
Keep me safe from the trap that
Has been set for me;
Shelter me from danger.
I place myself in your care.
You will save me, Lord;
You are a faithful God.

Litany of mercy

Leader: For the times we have doubted that you are there for us –

All: Oh God, we are sorry.

Leader: For the times we have not recognised each other's humanity –

All: Oh God, we are sorry.

Leader: For the times we have failed to rejoice in the gifts we have been given –

All: Oh God, we are sorry.

Leader: We ask for your forgiveness God –

All: And commit ourselves to living as humanly as we can.

Amen

Spontaneous prayers

Leader: We believe in a God of love who understands our daily frustrations and difficulties. We bring our concerns before you.

(Time for everyone to contribute prayers.)

Reading: Mark 4:35–41

On the evening of that same day, Jesus said to his disciples, 'Let us go across to the other side of the lake.' So they left the crowd; the disciples got into the boat in which Jesus was sitting and they took him with them. Other boats were there too. Suddenly a strong wind blew up, and the waves began to spill over into the boat, so that it was about to fill with water. Jesus was in the back of the boat, sleeping with his head on a pillow. The disciples woke him up and said, 'Teacher, don't you care that we are about to die?'

Jesus stood up and commanded the wind, 'Be quiet!' and he said to the waves, 'Be still!' The wind died down, and there was great calm Then Jesus said to his disciples, 'Why are you frightened? Have you still no faith?'

Leader: We have probably all had times when we have felt as overwhelmed as Daniel and Katie. Perhaps because of injustice, or perhaps due to other factors. At such times, have we turned to God, or have we let our fears overcome us. Do we believe God will be there to calm the wind eventually?

(Short period of reflection from the group.)

Leader: Let us all join together in the closing prayer.

Closing Prayer
Prayer in time of trouble

Lord, in every need let me come to You with humble
   trust saying, 'Jesus, help me.'
In all my doubts, perplexities, and temptations, Jesus,
   help me.
In hours of loneliness, weariness, and trials, Jesus, help
   me.
In the failure of my plans and hopes; in disappointments,
   troubles, and sorrows, Jesus, help me.
When others fail me and Your grace alone can assist
   me, help me.
When I throw myself on Your tender love as a father
   and saviour, Jesus, help me.
When my heart is cast down by failure at seeing no
   good come from my efforts, Jesus, help me.
When I feel impatient and my cross irritates me, Jesus,
   help me.
When I am ill and my head and hands cannot work and
   I am lonely, Jesus, help me.
Always, always, in spite of weakness, falls, and
   shortcomings of every kind, Jesus, help me and
   never forsake me.
Amen

Anonymous, published on beliefnet.com

ACT
(10 mins)

> 'What does the Lord require of you, but to act justly, to love mercy, and to walk humbly with your God?' (Micah 6:8)

The above line from scripture inspires many activists who work for justice and peace, particularly when we reflect on people experiencing oppression.

Over the next week, take the time to try and live this in your daily life. Discuss these questions as a group and then think how you might implement them.

- How can you act justly to your family? To your co-workers? To people you meet?
- How do you ensure that you are merciful to people you encounter?
- What does it mean to walk humbly with your God?

FURTHER REFLECTION

In this session we have been thinking about how we might try and maintain our humanity living under an oppressive regime. But what happens afterwards? When you are finally released from your anguish? Or when the regime is no more? How do you stay human then?

For some people, the experience is so destructive, their lives will never the same again. Paddy Hill was one of the Birmingham Six. Wrongly accused of planting the 1974 Birmingham bomb that killed 21 people and injured 162 others, Hill was beaten up by the police, threatened with a gun and eventually convicted along with five other men, mainly on the basis of false confessions. They were to spend sixteen years in prison before finally being released in 1991. The men were released without being given counselling. This has been particularly hard on Hill, who still struggles with the trauma he endured, to such an extent that he dreams of killing policemen, cannot forgive his captors and finds it difficult to maintain relationships with the people he loves. He attributes his current problems to the lack of professional help he received on his release.[4]

For others, it seems possible to find a way through the trauma. The whistleblower Chelsea Manning, who released evidence of US war crimes in Iraq, was often treated harshly in prison, being placed in solitary confinement and not receiving appropriate support when she came out as transgender. However, her statement on leaving prison in May 2017 suggests someone whose aim is to turn her suffering into something positive:

'For the first time, I can see a future for myself as Chelsea. I can imagine surviving and living as the person who I am and can finally be in the outside world. Freedom used to be something that I dreamed of but never allowed myself to fully imagine. Now, freedom is something that I will again experience with friends and loved ones after nearly seven years of bars and cement, of periods of solitary confinement, and of my health care and autonomy restricted, including through routinely forced haircuts. I am forever grateful to the people who kept me alive, President Obama, my legal team and countless supporters.

'I watched the world change from inside prison walls and through the letters that I have received from veterans, trans young people, parents, politicians and artists. My spirits were lifted in dark times, reading of their support, sharing in their triumphs, and helping them through challenges of their own. I hope to take the lessons that I have learned, the love that I have been given, and the hope that I have to work toward making life better for others.'[5]

Similarly on a national scale we can see different responses to the end of a tyranny. In Romania, when the dictator Nicolae Ceausescu was deposed he and his wife Elena were found guilty of genocide in an hour-long trial whose outcome was predetermined. They were shot by firing squad the same day. While no one can dispute the horrors of the Romanian regime, the fact that the revolution resulted in deaths conducted in this way suggests that revenge, rather than justice was the motivating factor.[6]

Contrast this with the end of apartheid in South Africa. The African National Congress had for many years conducted an armed struggle against the apartheid regime. Many assumed that when this government was eventually overthrown it would be after a bloody and unpleasant war. However, not only did apartheid end peacefully after a long series of negotiations between the ANC and the de Klerk government, but instead of revenge, South Africa chose to set up a Truth and Reconciliation Commission. This allowed victims and perpetrators of violence to meet together in public hearings so that the truth could be known and there was a possibility of reconciliation between the parties.

There is no doubt the Truth and Reconciliation Commission was challenging and imperfect. Gillian Slovo, the daughter of ANC activists Joe Slovo and Ruth First, writes in her memoir of the shocking murder of her mother. When Joe Slovo later agreed to the Commission as part of the peace process, he knew that it meant Ruth's murderers would go free.[7] Gillian later wrote of the Commission that it had increased her hatred for Ruth's murderers because they were motivated by hatred. And yet, even though she couldn't reconcile with her mother's killers, the process helped her reconcile with what happened, and overall helped 'a whole society reconcile itself to its past, without ignoring or denying it.'[8]

Living in oppressive systems, individuals can be crushed, broken, beaten. They can emerge bitter and angry determined to wreak vengeance on those who hurt them. Or they can find ways to remain true to themselves, through the love of friends and family, a passion for justice, an ability to find a private place for themselves. And when the system is overthrown, they can choose the path of truth and reconciliation, however imperfect.

None of us know how we might react in such circumstances, but all of us perhaps know what we would wish to aspire to:

Then Peter came to Jesus and asked, 'Lord, how many times shall I forgive my brother or sister who sins against me? Up to seven times?' Jesus answered, 'I tell you, not seven times, but seventy-seven times.'

Matthew 18:21–22

NOTES FOR WEEK 2

1. 'Isis survivor Nadia Murad turns harrowing suffering into humanitarian initiative', Women in the World Staff, *New York Times*, 15th September 2016. https://nytlive.nytimes.com/womenintheworld/2016/09/15/isis-survivor-nadia-murad-turns-harrowing-personal-suffering-into-humanitarian-initiative/?mcubz=2

2. The Forgiveness Project: Camilla Carr and Jon James (England), 29th March 2010. http://theforgivenessproject.com/stories/camilla-carr-jon-james-england/

3. 'Was I reckless? No', Aida Eidemariam, *Guardian*, 10th May 2007. https://www.theguardian.com/politics/2007/mar/10/iraq.world1

4. 'Paddy Hill: "All I think about is shooting police. I am traumatised" ', Amelia Hill, *Guardian* 4th November 2010. https://www.theguardian.com/law/2010/nov/04/paddy-hill-birmingham-six-counselling

5. Chelsea Manning Release Statement, 9th May 2017. https://www.luminairity.com/chelsea-release-statement/

6. The Trial of Nicolae and Elena Ceausescu, Wikipedia. https://en.wikipedia.org/wiki/Trial_of_Nicolae_and_Elena_Ceau%C8%99escu

7. *Every Secret Thing: My Family, My Country*, Gillian Slovo, London: Abacus, 1997.

8. 'Making History. South Africa's Truth and Reconciliation Commission', Gillian Slovo, Open Democracy website, 5th December 2002.

week 3
COMPASSION IN THE DARKNESS

TO GET YOU STARTED

'Love your neighbour as yourself' is the second of the ten commandments, coming straight after 'Love the Lord your God with all your heart and all your strength'. Its proximity to the first suggests that after loving God, loving your neighbour is pretty central to Jewish, Islamic and Christian belief.

The parable of the Good Samaritan is Jesus' response to a challenge from a teacher of the law, 'who is my neighbour?' The story is familiar to most of us: a man is set upon by thieves and left for dead. First a priest, then a Levite (a religious tribe with special status, who often taught the law), see him lying on the ground. Not only do they do nothing, but they walk on by on the other side of the road, which seems deliberately cruel. It is the third passer-by, an outcast Samaritan, whose 'heart filled with pity'. He takes care of the man, dressing his wounds, settling him at an inn and paying for his keep.

The parable is a salutary one. We might expect that the priest and lawyer, men with high status who theoretically work for the good of all, would be quick to help. And yet they ignore the victim's suffering, deliberately turning their backs. When Jesus asks 'which one of these three acted like a neighbour?' the answer is obviously the man who showed kindness, the Samaritan. Jesus couldn't be clearer: we should be like the Samaritan, not the leaders. He instructs his challenger to 'go, then and do likewise'.

Jesus' message is that if we act like the priest or Levite in this story, we are failing in our responsibilities as Christians. Instead we are called to act with compassion, as Jesus does time and time again. How many times, in the Bible do we see him reach out to people whom society has ignored or despised – blind Bartimeus, disabled people, sex workers – with sensitivity and love? He frequently shows the disciples how it is done – not to judge, not to condemn, but to treat each human being with dignity and respect. It is clear that we are expected to do the same, but is it as simple as that?

As noted earlier, the story is told in answer to a question, who is my neighbour? While we are given an answer to that question, we never find out why the priest and Levite act differently. One reading of their behaviour is that perhaps they were in a hurry – and didn't have time to help. Another possible explanation is that they were overwhelmed by the situation and didn't feel able to help. A third interpretation is that choosing to walk by on the other side is a conscious decision not to assist, and in doing so, they choose to ally with the perpetrators of the crime, rather than the victim.

When we are faced with situations of injustice it is very common to be faced with all these responses. How often have we felt too busy to help someone? Or overwhelmed by the complexity of a situation so feel unable to offer assistance? And while many of us would hope we wouldn't deliberately walk by on the other side, there may be times when we've been complicit with injustice and suffering because doing something about it feels too difficult.

The other day I was travelling on a bus into town. A woman came on board who seemed in great distress. As the bus moved off, she began to moan in pain. At first no one responded, I think we were all hoping she would feel better. But the journey only made her feel worse. Eventually, a couple of us spoke to her. Initially, she said she was OK, so we sat back down. I have to confess I was relieved, because I had a lot to do when I was in town and not a lot of time. While I wanted to help her, I was worried that doing so might delay me. But, after a little while, she began to shout again. This time, the other person was up immediately, sat beside the woman, calmed her, made her laugh and then promised to stay with her till she met her friend. I was blown away by the young woman's kindness and compassion, and the impact it had on the woman who was distressed. Particularly, because I recognised in myself a strong desire not to be helpful. When I saw them later, sitting and chatting as if they were old friends, it served to remind me of what can happen if we respond to another's pain.

And yet, it is also not selfish to want to preserve something of ourselves, otherwise the pain of others is so great that it makes us feel helpless. Which is why if we are to act as Samaritans, we also need to remember the importance of having boundaries. In her brilliant book *Audacity to Believe*[1] Sheila Cassidy recounts how her imprisonment and subsequent torture in Chile during the Pinochet regime, woke her conscience to the poverty and struggles of others. When she returned to Britain, she originally tried to live as simply as possible in order to identify with those struggles. But gradually, she realised that not having a carpet, not having possessions, or a television was making her unable to function in her job as a doctor. She realised that in order to help others she needed to make sure she looked after herself too. She was right, because Jesus asks us to love our neighbour, *as ourselves*. That second part is as important as the first. Because if we don't love ourselves enough, we have no strength to love others. It is when we do both, that we are able to reach our hands out in compassion, and not pass by on the other side.

SeSSiON 3

THINK
(1 hr)

Clip 1, Scene 9, 1–5 minutes (till the end of the scene in the foodbank)

In this section Daniel accompanies Katie to the food bank. They join a long queue. In one of the most visceral scenes in the film, Katie, who has been starving herself to feed her children, cannot stop herself from opening a can of cold beans. She stuffs the food down and then breaks down. The food bank workers (all real volunteers) react with horror that she is in such a state of distress and then with kindness and sensitivity.

DISCUSSION
(10 minutes)

- How did you react when you saw this scene?
- Have you ever experienced food poverty? Can you imagine what that might be like? How would you want to be treated?
- Are you involved in a local food bank? Have you ever considered why so many food banks exist today?

Clip 2, Scene 11, 5-7 minutes (interview with DWP worker)

In an earlier scene that we watched last week Daniel experiences a similar moment of compassion, when he visits the job centre and sees the member of staff who had been kind to him the previous week. She is helping him, when her boss intervenes and tells her not to. In this scene we see Daniel meeting another job centre worker who has a different approach to his situation.

DISCUSSION
(15 minutes)

- Why does Daniel experience such different responses from the two job centre workers?
- Contrast this with the scene in the food bank. What is stopping the second DWP worker from behaving like the food bank volunteers?
- Do you have any sympathy with the DWP worker? What would you do if you had her job?

Thinking about both scenes:

- Where does compassion spring from? Is it something that can be taught?
- How did Jesus manage to be compassionate even on the Cross?

BROADER DISCUSSION
(25 minutes)

In 1977, Count Nikolai Tolstoy published a book, *The Secret Betrayal*[2] in which he documented a shameful moment in western history. Between 1943 and 1947 the British and American governments repatriated nearly two and a half million Soviet prisoners of war and refugees against their wishes and despite knowing that they would likely be ill-treated on their return. While the majority of soldiers complied with these orders some resisted. Those that followed orders were complicit in the imprisonment, deaths and torture that followed. Those that didn't helped the refugees escape.

Yugoslavian refugees were also subjected to the same treatment during this period. My brother-in-law's father, Roger Williams, was in a platoon given orders to repatriate people fleeing oppression in Yugoslavia. They were painfully aware of the Nuremberg Trials, and the knowledge that 'following orders' was no longer a sufficient reason not to help. Recognising the Yugoslavians as fellow human beings first, they refused the order, and saved lives, despite facing possible punishment themselves. Shortly afterwards Roger met and married a German woman, Rosemarie, with whom he had a long and very happy marriage, proving in the best way possible that there is always a human being beyond the idea of the 'enemy'.

In recent years in Europe we have seen large numbers of refugees fleeing wars. We have seen borders erected and many countries choosing to turn people back. Every day border staff are faced with the same dilemma Roger Williams faced, to let people cross or turn them back. Meanwhile, many who choose to help refugees are criminalised. In 2015, three Spanish firefighters working for an NGO were arrested in Greece after they rescued refugees from the sea. Despite receiving a great deal of support for their actions, they are facing trial for human trafficking, while other activists have been fined for giving refugees lifts or cups of coffee. [3]

- Were Roger and his colleagues right to ignore orders and let the Yugoslavians stay?
- Should we criminalise people who help refugees?
- Is there a limit to how open our borders can be? Is it right to follow orders to maintain them?
- Is there a Christian response to the refugee crisis?

PRAY
(20 minutes)

Reading: Luke 9:25-36

An expert in the law stood up to test Jesus. 'Teacher,' he asked, 'what must I do to inherit eternal life?'

'What is written in the Law?' he replied. 'How do you read it?'

He answered, 'Love the Lord your God with all your heart and with all your soul and with all your strength and with all your mind'; and, 'Love your neighbour as yourself.' 'You have answered correctly,' Jesus replied. 'Do this and you will live.'

But he wanted to justify himself, so he asked Jesus, 'And who is my neighbour?'

In reply Jesus said: 'A man was going down from Jerusalem to Jericho, when he was attacked by robbers. They stripped him of his clothes, beat him and went away, leaving him half dead. A priest happened to be going down the same road, and when he saw the man, he passed by on the other side. So too, a Levite, when he came to the place and saw him, passed by on the other side. But a

Samaritan, as he travelled, came where the man was; and when he saw him, he took pity on him.

He went to him and bandaged his wounds, pouring on oil and wine. Then he put the man on his own donkey, brought him to an inn and took care of him. The next day he took out two denarii and gave them to the innkeeper. "Look after him," he said, "and when I return, I will reimburse you for any extra expense you may have."

'Which of these three do you think was a neighbour to the man who fell into the hands of robbers?'

The expert in the law replied, 'The one who had mercy on him.'

Jesus told him, 'Go and do likewise.'

Litany of mercy

Leader: For the times we have lacked compassion –

All: Oh God, we are sorry.

Leader: For the times we have deliberately ignored suffering –

All: Oh God, we are sorry.

Leader: For the times we have let an injustice stand –

All: Oh God, we are sorry.

Leader: We ask for your forgiveness God –

All: And commit ourselves to becoming as compassionate we can.

Amen

Spontaneous prayers

Leader: Our God is a compassionate God. Slow to anger and abounding in love. We ask for your compassion Lord as we pray.

(Short time for people to pray.)

Reading: Matthew 25:35–40

I was hungry and you fed me, thirsty and you gave me a drink; I was a stranger and you welcomed me, naked and you clothed me. I was sick and you took care of me, in prison and you visited me.

Leader: We would all want to be compassionate to those who need our help. But sometimes we fail to act in kindness because of fear, exhaustion or our own burdens. How can we try and respond to Jesus' call for us to be generous and loving to all our fellow human beings?

(Short period of reflection.)

Closing Prayer
A prayer of compassion from Mother Theresa

Lord, open our eyes
that we may see you in our brothers and sisters.
Lord, open our ears
that we may hear the cries of the hungry,
the cold, the frightened, the oppressed.
Lord, open our hearts

that we may love each other as you love us.

Renew in us your spirit.

Lord, free us and make us one.

Amen

ACT
(10 minutes)

In 2013, vicar Keith Hebden initiated the UK End Hunger Fast project. Throughout Lent he, fellow minister, Simon Cross, and Catholic Worker Scott Albrecht, fasted in solidarity with those who faced hunger today. In doing so they brought attention to the rise of food banks and the causes of this, encouraging others to come together in a national day of fasting.

Have a conversation about the following actions you could take this week either as a group or individually:

- Take one day when you reduce food, or fast completely. Use the day in prayer to focus on the needs of those who go hungry in the UK and the world. Donate the money you save to a charity or campaign group acting to resolve hunger.
- OR, If you are unable to fast, help out at your local food bank, talk to the people who come and learn their stories.
- OR, Find out about what your local situation is, write to your local MP to raise awareness of people

going hungry in your area and ask them to make a stand about food poverty.

FURTHER REFLECTION

When I, Daniel Blake came out, most people responded with compassion and horror that in this day and age, people could be treated like this. Sadly, this response was not universal. Damien Green the then Secretary of State for the Department of Work and Pensions was quick to condemn the film[4] while journalists Camilla Long and Toby Young were incredulous that such things happened in modern Britain.[5]

Yet, as Paul Laverty, the writer of I, Daniel Blake pointed out – the film if anything, underplayed the problems, as they didn't want cinema goers to think they were exaggerating. There are far too many real Daniel Blakes out there and their stories are often even more tragic. In 2011 Chris and Helen Mullins committed suicide after living in poverty for eighteen months. With Helen being denied benefits, they had £57.50 a week, to live off. They were unable to heat their flat and with no food had to walk 12 miles to a soup kitchen to be fed. Eventually, they could not bear to live any longer.[6] In February 2014, Mark Woods, who had mental health needs, died of starvation, after his benefits were cut.[7] While Sheila Holt was made so anxious by being found fit for work that she was admitted to a psychiatric ward. There she had a heart attack that resulted in her going into a coma. Even then she received letters demanding she join the government's work programme. When she died in 2015, her father Ken blamed the government's WCA programme for causing her suffering which he said 'need not have happened.'[8]

The work capability assessment is not the only cruel part of the welfare system. As the film shows, Katie is forced to move out of London due to lack of affordable housing. Her children have to change schools, and she is without the support system and networks she grew up with. When things become harder for her, she has no one to rely on which forces her to make stark choices to feed her family. There are very many real Katies out there, as the combination of a cap on housing benefit and London councils selling off their housing estates has meant people are unable to afford local housing. Councils legally obliged to house homeless people often offer solutions a long way from home. While there have been many local campaigns such as Focus E15 in Newham, Save Cressingham Gardens in Lambeth and Sweets Way in Barnet,[9] many people remained unaware of this crisis until the tragic fire at Grenfell Tower in June 2017. This entirely avoidable disaster, created by a combination of cuts to regulation, a council seeking cheaper alternatives, and a landlord not fulfilling its obligations,[10] resulted in a huge death toll. With hundreds of people made homeless and some facing the prospect of moving out of the area, the tragedy has rightly caused many to question housing policy in Britain today.

Another key failure of the welfare system is the use of sanctions to penalise claimants. Katie's experience in the film, having her benefits cut because she was late, is all too common. Sanctions have been given to people for missing appointments due to attending funerals, or being ill, or finding time management difficult due to mental health needs.[11] Meanwhile other welfare changes such as the 'bedroom tax' which charges people in social housing extra for having a spare room, and the change from disability living allowance to personal independence payments, have also led to claimants losing money. And the new 'universal credit' that puts all benefits into one payment has been so poorly managed that many people end up with no income for weeks on end.[12] No wonder study after study has linked the rise of food banks with welfare cuts.[13]

For those of us who have been campaigning to end such suffering, the response of commentators such as Young and Long seems incredibly callous. How can they witness such suffering and not offer compassion? I had a similar emotion during the 2017 election campaign watching the Victoria Derbyshire programme. A young disabled activist spoke passionately about her situation and that of others, saying that people were dying because of government policy and nobody seemed to care. The majority of the audience responded in sympathy and horror, and yet the Conservative MP on the programme seemed unable to comprehend the scale of the problem. As I heard him attempt to dismiss her concerns and suggest that Labour's plans to improve the welfare system was a 'childish wish list', I found myself becoming very angry with him. How could he be so cold and hard when faced with the suffering in front of him?

After the programme I looked the MP up. He

lives in a wealthy part of Surrey, and it occurred to me that although the WCA is a universal system, its impacts are more widely felt in poorer areas. It is quite possible that he has simply not seen the harm that his government is doing, and perhaps chooses not to look outside the comfort of his own situation because it was too uncomfortable. And I was reminded of a comment from *To Kill A Mockingbird*. At the end of the trial, Atticus comforts his son that a man who only the night before was part of a mob wanting to kill the accused man, Tom Robinson, had fought for his acquittal. This was because, Atticus said, the family's challenge to mob mentality had 'disturbed him in his mind' and caused him to change it. It strikes me that perhaps for that MP that woman's challenge disturbed him in his mind. Perhaps his defensiveness was due to him being confronted with something so big he couldn't immediately see it. Perhaps it wasn't lack of compassion but lack of understanding, and that when he had time to reflect, perhaps he would begin to think differently.

And it maybe that the MP will begin to listen to some of his peers in the House of Commons, many of whom are showing unease not just with the WCA but other aspects of welfare reform. Just before the 2017 Conservative Party Conference, 12 back bench MPs called for a halt to Universal Credit, which is likely to make this bad situation worse[14]. This call was echoed by the former Prime Minister, John Major, who said the policy was 'socially unfair and unforgiving'. All of which suggests there is an increasing awareness within members of the government that society needs to be compassionate.[15] And when enough of us are compassionate enough, we will all be prepared to be Samaritans and our society will be better off for it.

NOTES FOR WEEK 3

1. *Audacity to Believe*, Sheila Cassidy, London: Darton, Longman and Todd, 1977.

2. Review of *Secret Betrayal*, by Nikolai Tolstoy, Charles Lutton, Institute for Historical Review, 1978. http://www.ihr.org/jhr/v1/v1n4p371_lutton.html

3. 'Spanish fire fighters who saved lives at sea must not be criminalised', Anya Edmond, Institute of Race Relations website, 18th May 2017. http://www.irr.org.uk/news/spanish-fire-fighters-who-saved-lives-at-sea-must-not-be-criminalised/

4. 'Ken Loach accuses government of "incompetence" after minister claims *I, Daniel Blake* is "monstrously unfair"', Katie Ferguson, *Independent*, 2nd November 2016. http://www.independent.co.uk/news/people/ken-loach-i-daniel-blake-damien-green-monstrously-unfair-a7393031.html

5. All Fur Coat and RA in chronic illness blog, 25th October 2016. https://allfurcoatandra.com/2016/10/26/i-daniel-blake-meets-haters-camilla-long-toby-young/

6. 'Army veteran and his wife die in tragic "suicide pact" after becoming "too poor to live through the winter"', Andy Dolan, *Daily Mail*, 9th November 2011. http://www.dailymail.co.uk/news/article-2059238/Army-veteran-Mark-Mullins-wife-Helen-driven-suicide-poverty.html

7. 'Vulnerable man starved to death after benefits were cut', Amelia Gentleman, *Guardian*, 28th February 2014. https://www.theguardian.com/society/2014/feb/28/man-starved-to-death-after-benefits-cut

8. 'Sheila Holt: woman ordered to find work while lying in a coma dies aged 48', Ros Wynne-Jones, *Daily Mirror*, 18th March 2015. http://www.mirror.co.uk/news/uk-news/ros-wynne-jones-sheila-hounded-death-5353202

9. *Foxes have their holes: Christian reflections on Britain's housing need*, Andrew Francis (editor), London: Ekklesia, 2016.

10. 'With Grenfell we've seen what "ripping up red tape" really looks like', George Monbiot, *Guardian*, 15th June 2017. https://www.theguardian.com/commentisfree/2017/jun/15/grenfell-tower-red-tape-safety-deregulation

11. 'Time to rethink benefit sanctions', Joint Public Issues Team, March 2015. http://www.jointpublicissues.org.uk/wp-content/uploads/rethink-sanctions-report-0315.pdf

12. 'The shrinking safety net', Bernadette Meaden, in *Reclaiming the Common Good: How Christians can help rebuild this broken world*, Virginia Moffatt (editor), London: Darton, Longman and Todd, 2017.

13. 'The link between benefit cuts and food banks' Naomi Rovnick, *Financial Times*, 28th October 2016.

14. 'Tory rebellion throws Universal Credit reforms into chaos', Christopher Hope, *Daily Telegraph*, 28th September, 2017 http://www.telegraph.co.uk/news/2017/09/28/universal-credit-roll-out-may-paused-head-rebellion-tory-mps/

15. 'Universal Credit "operationally messy, socially unfair and unforgiving" as ex-PM John Major latest Tory to slam the new system', *Mirror*, Nicola Bartlett, 8th October 2017.

Week 4
FIGHTING BACK OR GIVING IN?

TO GET YOU STARTED

As we saw in Week Two, there are many stories of oppression in the Bible. In Exodus, the Egyptians enslave the immigrant Israelites; in the book of Kings, the Israelites are held captive by the Babylonians; in Jesus' time, Israel was occupied by Rome. And because every human is different, we also witness different responses to ill treatment. Some have faith that God will ease their suffering:

> And it will be in the day when the Lord gives you rest from your pain and turmoil and harsh service in which you have been enslaved, that you will take up this taunt against the king of Babylon, and say, 'How the oppressor has ceased, And how fury has ceased!'
>
> Isaiah 14:3–4

While others despair that the evil will not be overcome:

How long shall the wicked, O Lord, How long shall the wicked exult? They pour forth words, they speak arrogantly; All who do wickedness vaunt themselves. They crush Your people, O Lord, And afflict Your heritage. They slay the widow and the stranger And murder the orphans. They have said, 'The Lord does not see, Nor does the God of Jacob pay heed.'

Psalm 94:3–7

The differences in approach may have been due to the time and circumstances of each writer. Isaiah's words were written as the Assyrian occupation was crumbling, when perhaps there was a real hope that change might come soon. This Psalm comes from a time at the beginning of the Babylonian invasion when things must have felt very bleak indeed and he must have felt abandoned by God. Neither state is right or wrong, after all, at his worst moment Jesus cried out 'My God, My God, why have you forsaken me?', but they indicate that people respond to enslavement in more than one way.

For example, when Moses is called by God to stand up for his people, he does, time and again. Though (and I rather like this as it shows heroes are not superhuman), he asks for Aaron to be his spokesperson, as he is not good at making speeches. Their resistance and persistence, coupled with the plagues that God sends, are in the end enough for Pharaoh to release the Israelites, even if he regrets the decision and sends his soldiers after the fleeing refugees.

Later on, David defeats the Philistine's fearsome warrior, the giant Goliath with a slingshot. Although the story is likely to be fiction, it can be seen as a metaphor for the idea that the weak can overcome the strong, or that the power of God is stronger than the power of evil.

Daniel is another biblical character we often associate with resistance, as he defied his king Nebuchadnezzar to continue praying. When the lions did not attack him, Daniel survived and returned to his place in court, interpreting the dreams of the king. Perhaps this was a pragmatic choice, but it does seem to be one of long-term collaboration for survival rather than ongoing resistance.

By Jesus' time, Israel was under Roman occupation again, with many anticipating the Messiah would rise up and overthrow the invaders. But Jesus' resistance was not a violent one. Rather than preaching violence to the occupiers, he taught a radical message of love for each other and the enemy. And, although some suggest ideas like 'turning the other cheek' imply passivity in the face of oppression, others interpret it as meaning that we should not respond to violence with violence.[1] In other words, Jesus was committed to non-violent resistance, a mission that marked him as an undesirable and led to his eventual arrest as a political prisoner and murder by the state.

These stories have often been inspirational for people in resistance movements. The slaves in the American south strongly identified with the slaves in

Egypt for example. Gandhi admired Jesus, quoting the Sermon on the Mount frequently, even if he was less admiring of Christians,[2] perhaps because they didn't always live up to Christ's words. Martin Luther King was inspired by Jesus and Gandhi suggesting that Jesus provided the inspiration, and Gandhi the techniques for nonviolent resistance.[3] Christian activists who today undertake acts of civil disobedience against militarism, or climate change, are similarly influenced, a common story cited being Jesus' own behaviour when he overturned the tables of the money lenders in the temple, which has been interpreted as an act of civil disobedience.[4]

However, there are also times when Christians appear to collaborate in order to survive. When Franz Jaegerstatter refused to fight in the Austrian army because of his opposition to Nazism, his own priest urged him to take up arms.[5] In France many women collaborated with Germans, sleeping with them or working for them,[6] leading to their condemnation and humiliating treatment after the war.[7] It is easy to join in the condemnation, but perhaps we should be careful, as who knows how we might have behaved in such circumstances? Perhaps Jaegerstatter's priest was fearful of reprisals for the village. Maybe the women had no resources to feed their family and felt they had no choice. Or perhaps, as the novelist Irène Némirovsky showed in her unfinished novel, *Suite Française*, love flourished between individuals who were afraid and found some human sympathy.[8]

Session 4

THINK
(1 hr)

Clip 1, Scene 14, 1–5 minutes (till Daniel is arrested)

By now we are a considerable way along in the film. Daniel has suffered set back upon set back. He has had to sell his possessions; he has very little money as he waits for his appeal to come through. He comes to the end of his tether, and in another iconic scene, spray paints a message on the side of the Job Centre. 'I, Daniel Blake demand an appeal date before I starve. And change the music on the phone, it's shite.' He sits and waits for the police to arrive, is arrested and release with a conditional discharge.

DISCUSSION
(10 minutes)

- What were your reactions to this scene?
- Do you think Daniel's action will change anything?
- Is his action pointless?

Clip 2, Scene 13, 1–4 minutes (till Katie sends him away)

Katie also comes to the end of her tether. After months of struggling to feed her children, she is caught stealing sanitary towels in a shop. The shopkeeper lets her off, but gives her his number. At first, she doesn't contact him, and then, when Daisy's shoes fall apart again, she is desperate and decides to become a sex worker. In this scene, we see Daniel discovering this and confronting her.

DISCUSSION

(15 minutes)

- How did you feel about the choice Katie makes? Why does she send Daniel away?
- What will her actions mean for her future and that of her children?
- Was there anything else she could have done?

Thinking about both scenes:

- Do you agree or disagree with Katie and Daniel's actions?
- Can you imagine acting as they did?

BROADER DISCUSSION

(25 minutes)

Throughout Jesus' ministry he is shown to have a close relationship with his followers. And yet, they all betray him in the end. Judas commits the act of treachery of going to Jesus' enemies and giving him up. Once Jesus is arrested everyone runs away. Even Peter, who promises never to leave Jesus, flees once he is confronted by people in the crowd. Though we all like to think we might be a hero in such circumstances, would reality test us and find us wanting?

In the novel *Silence*, Shusaku Endo[9] takes this idea and explores it through the experiences of two Jesuit priests who embark on a mission in seventeenth-century Japan to discover if their former mentor has apostasised. The book, which was recently made into a film by Martin Scorsese, follows the pair as they find their way into a society where Christianity is illegal and its adherents are tortured and murdered in the most brutal ways. The central character Fr Rodrigues must grapple with his faith and conscience and whether these matter if his refusal to recant means others suffer. It is a powerful insight into the grim realities of such a situation and provides us with a sense that the answers are not simple.

- Can you imagine living in such circumstances? How would it feel?
- Would you resist the system? If so, how?
- Why might collaboration be an option? Would you judge someone for collaborating?
- Do you think Christians have a particular responsibility to resist?

PRAY
(20 minutes)

Reading: Luke 23:54–62

They arrested Jesus and took him away into the house of the High Priest; and Peter followed at a distance. A fire had been lit in the centre of the courtyard, and Peter joined those who were sitting round it. When one of the servant women saw him sitting there at the fire, she looked straight at him and said, 'This man too was with Jesus!'

But Peter denied it, 'Woman, I don't even know him!' After a little while a man noticed Peter and said, 'You are one of them, too!' But Peter answered, 'Man, I am not!' And about an hour later another man insisted strongly, 'There isn't any doubt that this man was with Jesus, because he also is a Galilean.' But Peter answered, 'Man, I don't know what you are talking about!'

At once, while he was still speaking, a cock crowed. Jesus turned round and looked straight at Peter, and Peter remembered what Jesus had said to him. 'Before the cock crows tonight, you will have denied me thrice.' Peter went out and wept bitterly.

Litany of mercy

Leader: For the times we have failed to stand up for what is right –

All: Oh God, we are sorry.

Leader: For the times we have remained silent in the face of injustice –

All: Oh God, we are sorry.

Leader: For the times we betrayed people we love –

All: Oh God, we are sorry.

Leader: We ask for your forgiveness God –

All: And commit ourselves working for justice.
Amen

Spontaneous prayers

Leader: We pray for all those struggling with injustice, and ask that God gives them strength to carry on.

(The group offers spontaneous prayers.)

Reading: Mark 11:15–19

When they arrived in Jerusalem, Jesus went to the Temple and began to drive out all those who were buying and selling. He overturned the tables of the money changers and the stools of those who sold pigeons, and he would not let anything through the temple courtyards. He then taught the people, 'It is written in the Scriptures that God said, "My Temple shall be called a house of prayer for the people of the nations." But you have turned it into a den of thieves!'

Leader: The German theologian, Dietrich Bonhoeffer famously said, 'We are not to simply bandage the wounds of victims beneath the wheels of injustice, we are to drive a spoke into the wheel itself.' Let us share some thoughts about how we might do this.

(Short time for reflection.)

Closing Prayer

O God of true democracy, of justice and love, our hope
is in you.

We pray for our country, its leaders, the people and our
environment.

Grant that we all take up the challenge of building a just
nation, the poor being its very foundation, and that
we may be responsible for our earth and cosmos.

Like Jesus of the Gospel, fill our hearts with your Spirit
to be fully human by affirming the dignity of all as
we wish to live out our ministry of Justice and Peace.

Guide us to bring your justice and peace into our
parishes and our work places, to our families and
communities.

Be with each of us.

Gift us with openness, a listening heart and courage
to act justly and peacefully, to love tenderly and
walk humbly with You our God.

We ask this through our Lord Jesus, our Friend and
Model.

Amen

From *Modern Prayers for Africa and the World*,
Missionaries of Africa, South Africa, by Fr Michel
Meunier

ACT

(10 minutes)

On the 15 July 2017, a group of Christians came
together to launch the Faith and Resistance Network.

The network offers support and solidarity to Christians wishing to engage in nonviolent direct action.

As a group, discuss what you think about direct action. Follow this up during the week by taking a look at the Faith and Resistance Network and Waging Nonviolence websites (details can be found in the resources section). Undertake one of the following actions:

- If you are interested in finding out more about nonviolent direct action get in touch with the network,
- OR find out ways to support those who undertake nonviolent direct action,
- OR pray for those doing this work.

FURTHER REFLECTION

In this section we have reflected on how people react to situations of injustice. So far the discussion has focused on people living in an unjust environment, and how they might resist. The majority of us are unlikely to experience such difficulties, but it is still possible to respond to the sins of government even if we are not directly affected. I have already talked at length about the problems created by the welfare system in modern Britain. But there are other areas where our government's decisions harm people, and sometimes, because the victims aren't in this country we might not even be aware of their suffering

Nuclear weapons, militarism and the arms trade are all areas that have a negative impact on the world. The threat of the destructive power of nuclear weapons has been hanging over us since the end of the Second World War, but even if they are not used, the vast expense spent on creating such weapons means there is less to spend on health, social care, education and housing.[11] Since the Gulf War in 1991, the US and Britain have fought wars in Iraq, Afghanistan, Libya and now Syria that have had terrible consequences for those countries, destroying the infrastructure and creating immense hardship and poverty[12] while the arms trade results in countries vying with each other to buy increasingly harmful bombs and bullets that cause misery across the globe.[13]

In 1980, a group of Christians, including veteran activists Daniel and Philip Berrigan, broke into a nuclear missile facility in Pennsylvania. Inspired by Isaiah's prophecy, 'they shall beat their swords into ploughshares, and their spears into pruning hooks' (Isaiah 2:4), they disarmed the nose cones of nuclear warheads with household hammers, and poured blood on documents, calling on the government to end nuclear proliferation.[14] Since then there have been many such actions across the world carried out by activists of all faiths and none.

Perhaps, the most well-known action in Britain took place in January 1996 at a factory in Warton run by the arms company British Aerospace Systems. Three women, Jo Blackman, Andrea Needham and

Lotte Kronlid entered the base and disarmed a Hawk Jet that was bound for Indonesia, where it would have been used to attack the people of East Timor. A fourth woman, Angie Zelter, was arrested a week later, after she publicly declared she too would be disarming a Hawk Jet. All four were charged with conspiracy to commit criminal damage, and the three who entered Warton, with criminal damage. At the time of their action East Timor had been living under a brutal Indonesian occupation for twenty one years. Over a third of the population had been killed, many more were imprisoned and tortured and the remainder lived in fear of bombing raids. Despite evidence of the suffering of the civilians of East Timor, and protests by British citizens, the British government signed a deal to sell the jets to Indonesia claiming that they were for training purposes.

At their subsequent trial, the four women were able to present evidence of the appalling situation East Timorese people lived in, including the Santa Cruz massacre in 1991. They brought in military experts who demonstrated that the Hawk jet was both a trainer jet and an active military jet, and provided evidence that Hawk jets had been responsible for bombing villages in East Timor. Perhaps the most powerful moment in the trial came from the witness Jose Ramos Horta, the then East Timorese ambassador in exile, who was asked what would have happened if someone in East Timor had tried to disarm the plane. His answer that they would be shot, demonstrating why sometimes it is necessary for people outside an oppressive situation to resist it, when those inside cannot. As a result of such testimony and the women's argument that they were acting to prevent the crime of genocide, the jury acquitted them. It was an amazing moment in British history, and as Jo said outside court, it was 'a great day for justice, a great day for the people of East Timor'.[15]

Shortly before the Seeds of Hope action, my husband and I attended a lobby of MPs at the House of Commons calling for a ban on the Hawk deal. I remember sitting in a talk afterwards feeling desperate about the plight of East Timor, wondering if the people would ever be free. The situation seemed hopeless, yet within three years of that meeting, the Indonesian regime had crumbled, allowing the UN to oversee the first free elections in East Timor since the invasion. Thirteen years later, while my daughter Claire and I were watching the Olympic men's marathon in London we noticed the penultimate runner was from East Timor. As he ran the final lap, an hour or so behind the winners, wrapped in a Timorese flag, the crowd chanted 'Timor, Timor', a powerful reminder to me that change is always possible.[16]

This January, twenty one years after the Seeds of Hope action, Sam Walton, a Quaker, and Daniel (Woody) Woodhouse, a Methodist minister, also broke into Warton, with the intent of disarming a plane bound for Saudi Arabia.[17] Although the pair did not reach their target, they were arrested and charged with two counts of criminal damage and, at the time of writing, face a trial later in the year. Like the Seeds of Hope women before them, Sam and Woody's action was a direct response to another sordid UK arms deal, this time with Saudi Arabia.

Saudi Arabia has been the British government's biggest arms customer since the 1960s. While the deals prove lucrative for companies such as British Aerospace, it has a devastating impact on civilians. Since 2015, Saudi Arabia has bombed its poverty stricken neighbour, Yemen, killing thousands of civilians and devastating the country. The bombings have damaged infrastructure so that only 45 per cent of hospitals survive, and have led to the spread of disease, malnutrition in children, 18.8 million people requiring humanitarian aid, and 3.1 million internally displaced citizens.[18] Despite this, the UK continues to deal with Saudi Arabia, and once more British Aerospace is only too happy to oblige by selling weapons.

On the 10th July 2017 as Sam and Woody made their way to court to find out their trial date, the campaign group, Campaign Against the Arms Trade (CAAT) was dealt a blow in the High Court. CAAT had taken out a judicial review to overturn the government's deal with Saudi Arabia, stating that it was illegal due to the suffering inflicted on the civilian population. Sadly, despite their strong moral and legal case, the government was able to persuade the judges with evidence produced in secret, that the Saudi Arabian government was doing all it could to protect Yemeni citizens. It is horrifying to realise that evidence provided behind closed doors is deemed more worthy than the evidence of report after report of the humanitarian crisis in Yemen.[19] Such days are disheartening for activists, and even more so for the innocent victims thousands of miles away. It is enough to make us despair and give up.

And yet the New Testament is a story of hope. John's Gospel begins with these words:

> In the Beginning was Word,
> The Word was with God.
> He was with God in the beginning.
> Through him all things came into being,
> Not one thing came into being except through him.
> What has come into being in him was life,
> Life that was the light of men;
> And light shines in the darkness,
> And darkness could not overpower it.
>
> John 1:1–5

The passage reminds us that we are people of the light. It is our duty to shine that light in the dark places to expose evil. We know that although we will sometimes feel the burden of the dark, it cannot, in the end, overpower the light. And the day will come, at some future Olympics, when a Yemenese athlete will run the marathon, knowing their country is free from war, to the cries of 'Yemen, Yemen, Yemen.' May that day come soon.

NOTES FOR WEEK 4

1. 'How Walter Wink confronted violence', Ken Butigan, Waging Nonviolence website, 17th May 2012. https://wagingnonviolence.org/feature/how-walter-wink-confronted-violence/

2. 'Mahatma Gandhi admired Jesus and his teachings but did not follow "Christianity" ', Kosarajuraj blog. http://kosarajuraj.blogspot.co.uk/2014/01/mahatma-gandhi-admired-jesus-and-his.html

3. 'Martin Luther King Junior: A history', Russel Moldovan, *Christianity Today*, 1st January 2000. http://www.christianitytoday.com/ct/2000/januaryweb-only/11.0b.html

4. 'The market is king', Keith Hebden. Text of sermon given at St Paul's Cathedral on 30th November 2014, reprinted on Resistance and Renewal website. https://resistanceandrenewal.net/2014/12/03/the-market-is-king-by-keith-hebden/

5. 'The two faces of wartime Germany, Hans Frank and Franz Jaegerstatter', Francis Phillips, *Catholic Herald*, 23rd May 2014. http://www.catholicherald.co.uk/commentandblogs/2014/05/23/the-two-faces-of-wartime-germany-hans-frank-and-franz-jagerstatter/

6. 'The women in World War 2 Paris who "did what they had to" for survival', Jenni Frazer, *The Times of Israel*, 2nd September 2016. http://www.timesofisrael.com/the-women-in-wwii-paris-who-did-what-they-had-to-for-survival/

7. 'An ugly carnival', Antony Beevor, *Guardian*, 5th June 2009. https://www.theguardian.com/lifeandstyle/2009/

jun/05/women-victims-d-day-landings-second-world-war

8. *Suite Française*, Irène Némirovsky, London: Chatto and Windus, 2006.

9. *Silence*, Shusaku Endo, London: Peter Owen, 1966.

10. Faith and Resistance Network. https://faithandresistance blog.wordpress.com/

11. How much does Trident cost? Full Fact website, 14th July 2016. https://fullfact.org/economy/trident-nuclear-cost/

12. 'Unworthy victims. Western wars have killed four million Muslims since 1990', Nafeez Ahmed, Stop the War Coalition website, 16th June 2017. http://www.stopwar. org.uk/index.php/news-comment/2615-unworthy-victims-western-wars-have-killed-four-million-muslims-since-1990

13. 'An introduction to the arms trade' CAAT website. https://www.caat.org.uk/issues/introduction

14. 'The Plowshares Eight: Thirty years on' Mary Ann Muller and Anna Brown, Waging Nonviolence website, 9th September 2010. https://wagingnonviolence.org/feature/the-plowshares-8-thirty-years-on/

15. 'The hammer blow' Andrea Needham, *Peace News*, 2016.

16. 'Olympics, politics and me' Virginia Moffatt, *Peace News*, September 2012. https://www.peacenews.info/node/6923/olympics-politics-and-me

17. 'Two arrested over "disarming warplanes at BAE Systems"', BBC News website, 29th January 2017. http://www.bbc. co.uk/news/uk-england-lancashire-38787630

18. 'The impact of the war in Yemen' CAAT Website. https://www.caat.org.uk/campaigns/stop-arming-saudi/yemen.

19. 'UK arms exports to Saudi Arabia can continue, High Court rules' Alice Ross, *Guardian*, 10th July 2017. https://www.theguardian.com/world/2017/jul/10/uk-arms-exports-to-saudi-arabia-can-continue-high-court-rules.

week 5

THE SUFFERING SERVANT

TO GET YOU STARTED

As many were aghast at him
– he was so humanly disfigured
that he no longer looked like a man –
so many nations will be astonished
and kings will stay tight-lipped before him,
seeing what had never been told them,
learning what they had not heard before.
Who has given credence to what we have heard?
And who has seen the revelation of Yahweh's
     arm?
Like a sapling he grew up before him,
like a root in arid ground.
He had no form or charm to attract us,
no beauty to win our hearts;
he was despised, the lowest of men,
a man of sorrows, familiar with suffering,
one from whom, as it were, we averted our gaze,
despised, for whom we had no regard.
Yet ours were the sufferings he was bearing,
ours the sorrows he was carrying,

while we thought of him as someone being
    punished
and struck with affliction by God;
whereas he was being wounded for our rebellions,
crushed because of our guilt;
the punishment reconciling us fell on him,
and we have been healed by his bruises.

                         Isaiah 52:14–53:5

The prophecy of the suffering servant, foretold in Isaiah and revealed in the torture and death of Jesus, is a harrowing one. The idea of a man so disfigured that he looks inhuman, is ugly, and despised so much that we 'averted our gaze', tells an important truth about suffering. It is ugly, and painful, making it easy to look away.

This is a common reaction to the ill-treatment of others, as articulated in the poem 'Musée des Beaux Arts' by W. H. Auden. The poet is reflecting on a painting by Brueghel, of the fall of Icarus. He notes how suffering takes place while ordinary life is going on, and is easily ignored; while someone is being tortured, a dog is running about as dogs do, a horse of the torturer is relieving an itch on a tree. The poem ends with the description of a ploughman looking away at the sight of Icarus falling, ignoring his anguish because it was not important, a boat sails by oblivious because it has somewhere to get to. It's a pessimistic view of the world, written at a time in 1939, just before the Second World War, when there was much to be pessimistic about. And today, it often seems as if there is too much pain in the world, so much so that we can become inured to it. Like the ploughman at the end of the poem we look away because it is not important enough to us, or because we cannot bear to watch.

Every Palm Sunday and Good Friday, when we re-live the story of Jesus' arrest, trial, torture and death, we are reminded that not only did he live and suffer as a human, he endured the worst possible examples of 'man's inhumanity to man'.

We can have several responses to Jesus' torment. We can 'avert our gazes', and avoid the story unless we have to, focusing instead on the resurrection that follows. We can duck the darkness of Holy Week and go straight to the joy of Easter. We can go in the opposite direction, and over-identify with Jesus' suffering, physically or mentally flagellating ourselves for our sins. We can draw comfort from the knowledge that having suffered like this, God truly understands our own suffering and is with us in times of difficulty. Or we can believe, as Jesus does on the cross, that he has forsaken us. Finally, we can recognise that the arrest, torture and crucifixion of Jesus reflect an ugly truth about the world. Throughout history governments and political groups have oppressed citizens in this way and continue to do so today. Our Christian response can also be to recognise this and stand up against oppression whenever we see it.

In reality, most of us have probably had all the above reactions. When images of war, death or torture come on our TV screens or Facebook page it is easy to switch off or mute the post so we don't have to see it. How many of us have used Lenten denial to demonstrate our piety and self-sacrifice? In times of darkness, we have probably both cursed and been comforted by God. And we can all sign a petition or attend a vigil in response to a situation of injustice.

This fifth and final session will be the last before Holy Week. It therefore provides us with an opportunity to prepare ourselves for our annual reflection on the suffering and death of Jesus. It is a time to ask ourselves why are people ill-treated, tortured, imprisoned, put to death? Why does God let this happen? Is there any meaning in suffering? What can we do to alleviate it?

Session 5

THINK
(1 hr)

As we have seen throughout this course, both Daniel and Katie suffer an enormously in this film, enduring humiliation, poverty, lack of control. In this last session, we will reflect on the tragic end to Daniel's story.

Clip 1, Scene 14, 7–10 minutes (till Daniel opens the door)

In this section we discover that Daniel has reached rock bottom. The cheerful friendly man who walked through the streets at the beginning of the film, joking with people and challenging his neighbours to put out their rubbish, is replaced by someone who has hidden from the world. Alone in his flat, he ignores Daisy ringing at the door, until she eventually persuades him to open it.

DISCUSSION
(10 minutes)

- How did you feel when you watched this part of the film?
- Why do you think Daniel is reacting like this?
- Have you ever felt such despair? How did you recover?

(Note to the leader – this might be difficult for some people, particularly those who have experienced serious depression, so do consider mentioning that before you start).

Clip 2, Scene 15, 1–4 minutes (until Katie finds Daniel dead)

In this clip, we see things have improved. Daniel is back to his old self as Katie accompanies him to his appeal hearing. We dare to hope that things might turn out all right for him. And then, just as he is in the toilet, he collapses. Katie and his lawyer rush in to find him dead.

DISCUSSION
(15 minutes)

- How did you feel at the beginning of the scene?
- What was your reaction to Daniel's death?
- How must Katie have felt?

(Note to leader – again please be sensitive with this part, particularly if anyone in the group has been recently bereaved.)

Thinking about both scenes:

- Why do you think Daniel died? Could his death have been prevented?
- Do you believe God allows suffering? If so, why?

BROADER THINKING
(25 minutes)

The film ends with Daniel's funeral. Katie speaks about her friend and reads the statement he would have made to the tribunal:

'I am not a client, a customer, nor a service user. I am not a shirker, a scrounger, a beggar nor a thief. I am not a national insurance number, nor a blip on a screen. I paid my dues, never a penny short, and was proud to do so. I don't tug the forelock but look my neighbour in the eye. I don't accept or seek charity. My name is Daniel Blake, I am a man, not a dog. As such I demand my rights. I demand you treat me with respect. I, Daniel Blake, am a citizen, nothing more and nothing less. Thank you.'

The quest to be treated as a citizen is a cry against injustice that has been heard throughout human history. From Moses to the Saudi Arabian prisoner of conscience Raif Badawi, from the civil rights movement in the USA to sick and disabled people in the UK today, people have stood up and demanded the right to be treated as an equal, with dignity and respect.

- What does it mean to be a citizen?
- What happens to a society when some are excluded from citizenship?
- Can you think of examples of people not being treated as full citizens in Britain today?
- How should Christians react when people are denied their human rights?

PRAY
(20 minutes)

Reading: Isaiah 53:6–53:12

See, my servant will act wisely;
We all, like sheep, have gone astray,
each of us has turned to our own way;
and the Lord has laid on him

the iniquity of us all.
He was oppressed and afflicted,
yet he did not open his mouth;
he was led like a lamb to the slaughter,
and as a sheep before its shearers is silent,
so he did not open his mouth.
By oppression and judgment he was taken away.
Yet who of his generation protested?
For he was cut off from the land of the living;
for the transgression of my people he was punished.
He was assigned a grave with the wicked,
and with the rich in his death,
though he had done no violence,
nor was any deceit in his mouth.
Yet it was the Lord's will to crush him and cause
      him to suffer,
and though the Lord makes his life an offering for sin,
he will see his offspring and prolong his days,
and the will of the Lord will prosper in his hand.
After he has suffered,
he will see the light of life and be satisfied;
by his knowledge my righteous servant will
      justify many,
and he will bear their iniquities.
Therefore I will give him a portion among the great,
and he will divide the spoils with the strong,
because he poured out his life unto death,
and was numbered with the transgressors.
For he bore the sin of many,
and made intercession for the transgressors.

Litany of mercy

Leader: For the times we have allowed our sufferings to totally dominate our lives –

Response: Oh God we are sorry.

Leader: For the times we have given in to despair –

Response: Oh God we are sorry.

Leader: For the times we have rejected the love of others –

Response: Oh God we are sorry.

Leader: We ask for your forgiveness –

Response: And commit ourselves to living fully.

Spontaneous prayers

Leader: We remember those who live with depression, who are are bereaved, or watching someone they love in pain. We ask that you are with them God, and comfort them in their suffering.

(Spontaneous prayers are offered.)

Reading: Matthew 11:28–31

Come to me, all you who are weary and heavy laden, and I will give you rest. Take my yoke and put it on you, and learn from me, for I am gentle and humble in spirit; and you will find rest. For my yoke is easy and my burden is light.

Leader: When we are in the middle of a difficult situation, it can sometimes be hard to see the light, to think that things might get better. At such times, we can feel God has abandoned us. Has this ever happened to you or anyone you know? How did you/they get through it?

A short period for people to offer reflections.

Closing prayer
Prayer for God's comfort and strength in times of need

Father, how I thank You that Jesus is my good Shepherd and is there to comfort and strengthen in times of suffering, sadness, pain and loss. Thank You that Your rod and staff sustain and keep me, no matter what season of life I am passing through and no matter how difficult the times become.

I praise You Lord, for You are my strong tower, into Whose everlasting arm I flee for protection and safety, for You have pledged to uphold me with the right hand of Your righteousness. Thank You that in the midst of suffering and distress You have undertaken never to leave me nor forsake me – and when I face times of loneliness and isolation, Your promised grace is sufficient to carry me through.

Lord I know that as Your child I am indeed blessed and to be able to rest in You as my daily companion, my faithful comforter and my wise counsellor. Thank You for bringing me to this point in my life and for so patiently teaching me the lesson of Your never-failing faithfulness.

Use me I pray, to give like-comfort, companionship and counsel to others who also need the strength of their good and faithful Shepherd and continue I pray, to uphold and teach me more of Your comfort and strength, grace and love, in Jesus name I pray, **Amen**

Reproduced with permission from
www.knowing-jesus.com

ACT
(10 minutes)

Ken Loach and Paul Laverty made the film *I, Daniel Blake* as a response to the harm created by the work capability assessment. Story telling is a technique many organisations and campaign groups use to raise awareness of an injustice. In 2011, Lisa Chalkley, a mental health activist, and I began the Atos Stories Collective as a way of challenging Atos Healthcare, a private company appointed by Labour to manage the work capability assessment at the time. We asked for people's experiences to help us create a play which could be performed by anyone, anywhere to inform the public about what was happening. The result was *Atos Stories*, a play for performance inspired by these statements, and *The Atos Monologues* which used the direct text from participants. The work was freely downloadable. The play was performed by the Newham theatre group, Act Up! Newham, who performed *Atos*

Stories in 2012. The *Monologues* were used by many groups and read as part of vigils, demonstrations and performances. The project culminated in 2013 with a mass read which happened both on the streets of Oxford and Lampeter and online with stories shared by livestreaming, podcast and on twitter.[1]

Take an issue you care about such as welfare cuts, homelessness, refugees, and find a project that has published real life experiences about this subject (some examples are given in the resources section at the end). Depending on the amount of time you have available, as a group either:

- Plan a public event to read these stories,
- OR share these stories via your social media accounts,
- OR tell other people about them..

FURTHER REFLECTION

In this week's session we have seen how Daniel was plunged into depths of despair, very similar to that experienced by Job:

> Human life is like forced army service
> Like a life of hard manual labour,
> Like slaves longing for cool shade;
> Like workers waiting for their pay.
> Month after month I have nothing to live for;
> Night after night brings me grief.

When I lie down to sleep, the hours drag.
I toss all night and long for dawn.

Job 7:1–4

Job's experience is a painful one, but fortunately it ends in joy and triumph as God rewards him for his faith. The story of Jesus' arrest, torture and crucifixion is far worse, and for the disciples, his death must have been the most harrowing experience. Every Palm Sunday, every Good Friday we are taken step by step through the betrayal, the suffering, the death and the desolation. Jesus' friends did not know on Good Friday, as we do, that Jesus would rise again, giving us the hope of the Resurrection to look forward to. The moment he gave up his spirit must have felt like the end of the world.

We are drawn into these events because the Bible tells it as a story and we can identify with the main character, Jesus and his followers. Good storytelling always does this, inviting us to participate in events, and side with the central figures. Which is why in the film we feel every moment of Daniel's despair, and the sadness which Katie cannot help. We feel hopeful when he recovers and attends his appeal, and are as devastated as Katie is when he dies. And yet, the defiance with which Katie speaks his words at the funeral, inspires us to want to make sure that no one else suffers like this again. The film also reveals an important truth about friendship, because it is through Katie's friendship that Daniel is able to gather his strength to carry on. It is

Daniel's friendship that gives Katie the ability to speak at his funeral.

As I mentioned in the introduction, reading the story of David Groves' tragic death, and the grief and anger of his family was the start of my involvement in the campaign against the work capability assessment (WCA). There were many people already there before me, protesting about the WCA and other aspects of welfare, particularly campaign groups such as Disabled People Against Cuts and Black Triangle. Members of both these organisations have experienced the WCA, seen friends and family go through it, and witnessed many who have died, some of whom are remembered at the website Calum's List[2]. BlackTriangle and DPAC have led frequent protests outside the Houses of Parliament while Pat's Petition and the WoW Petition, used the government's petition processes to challenge these issues in the House of Commons.

But, despite their grief and anger, over the last few years, activists have not given up. In fact, it is their support and solidarity for each other, that has kept them going. I have been at several demonstrations during this time and I am always struck by the way activists support each other with humour, encouragement, and finding creative ways to challenge the government. It is this passion and determination that has helped make the WCA so politically toxic that all the major parties except the Conservatives now reject it, with many Conservative back benchers (such as Heidi Allen) being highly critical.

One WCA campaigner I knew was a woman called Karen Sherlock. Karen and I never met in real life, but we spoke regularly on twitter. Karen had a heart condition, kidney failure and was receiving dialysis treatment three times a week. Despite this she was found fit for work. Like many other people she kept campaigning, recounting for us the many absurdities she encountered in the system, and telling us she would be appealing against her result. She was often stressed and anxious and yet she was always ready to offer support to people in need. She was forthright and focused on the campaign, determined that she would win her appeal. And on 31st May 2012, she was able to share the good news that she had won. It had been a long battle and we were all delighted to celebrate with her. So it was a huge shock, a week later on the 8th June, when her husband Nigel sent a message from her twitter account to say that she had died.[3]

Of all the many horror stories that I have read since 2011, it is Karen's that has affected me most deeply. Throughout her suffering, I observed her grit and determination, her humour and her ability to care for others. So the irony of her death, so soon after she had achieved her aim, was hard to witness. And the stoicism and love her husband Nigel expressed only served to make me admire them both even more.

It is impossible to say whether the stress of appealing her WCA decision contributed to Karen's death, but given how ill she was, it cannot have helped. And it is sobering to know that between 2011 and 2014,

2,380 people died after they were found fit to work. In the same period 7,200 more people died after they were found fit for work-related activity.[4] Although we should be cautious about a direct causal link between the outcome of the assessment and the deaths, it is shocking that people this ill were placed in a situation where they were expected to work, or undertake work-related activity. No wonder a 2015 UN investigation into welfare reform found the British government had 'gravely violated' the rights of sick and disabled people.[5]

At the time of writing, it feels as if the situation might finally be changing. Six years ago, the WCA had broad political support, now the only party that backs it is the Conservative party. Over the last two years, the think tank Ekklesia undertook research with sick and disabled people to identify what the main problems with the WCA are in order to propose how the system could be redesigned.[6,7,8] Meanwhile Dr Simon Duffy of the Centre for Welfare Reform has spent the last seven years developing positive ideas for a welfare system[9] based on the rights of citizens and offering basic income.[10] With the Conservatives hanging onto power by their finger nails, I am very hopeful that the WCA and welfare reform will soon be confined to the past. When they are, we will look back at the success of a campaign that involved direct action, vigils, petitions, letter writing, lobbying MPs, but began when people started to tell their stories. We will remember that stories have the power to change the world if we want them to.

As we enter Holy Week we will witness the hardest part of Jesus' story, the torment and suffering that will lead to the moment of deep despair. We will follow Jesus every step of the way because we know that in doing so we will understand anew that we are called to act in solidarity with all who suffer and are oppressed. We know that after the horror of Jesus' death, we will witness the resurrection anew. And we will be reminded that when we commit ourselves to working with others for justice we will bring about the kingdom of God that John the Baptist predicted.

NOTES FOR WEEK 5

1.   'End ESA now' Write to Protest (formerly Atos Stories) blog, 19th March 2013. http://atosstories.blogspot.co.uk/2013/03/esa-end-game_19.html

2.   Calum's List. http://calumslist.org/

3.   'RIP Karen Sherlock' Sue Marsh, Diary of a Benefit Scrounger blog, 11th June 2012. https://diaryofabenefitscrounger.blogspot.co.uk/2012/06/rip-karen-sherlock.html

4.   'Thousands have died after being found fit for work, DWP figures show', Patrick Butler, *Guardian*, 27th August 2015.

5.   'UN: "Grave" disability rights violations under UK reforms', BBC News website, 7th November 2016. http://www.bbc.co.uk/news/uk-37899305

6.   'Determining the support need of people with chronic illness' Stef Benstead, Ekklesia, 28th July 2016. http://www.ekklesia.co.uk/ESAreportPartOne

7.   'Replacing Employment Support Allowance' Stef Benstead, Ekklesia, 1st October 2016. http://www.ekklesia.co.uk/sites/ekklesia.co.uk/files/ekklesia_esa_report2_oct_2016.pdf

8.   Forthcoming from Ekklesia, proposals for replacing employment support allowance.

9.   Centre for Welfare Reform website. http://www.centreforwelfarereform.org/

10. 'A new vision for welfare', Simon Duffy in *Reclaiming the Common Good: How Christians can help rebuild our broken world*, Virginia Moffatt (editor), London: Darton, Longman and Todd, 2017.

CONCLUSION

Over the last five weeks we have taken the time to look at one film, *I, Daniel Blake* and examine how the story of two people struggling with the UK benefits system might have something to say to us during Lent.

The film, and the real life stories that inspired it, highlights a very sorry period in our history, one where our politicians have been so focused on the ideology of austerity, that they abandoned people who are in most need. As mentioned in the previous chapter, I am hopeful that because of all the stories told and campaign actions taken we are on the cusp of real change, and we will see the end of the WCA and other welfare reforms.

Although I am confident that we will eventually win this fight, I know there will be other situations of injustice that will trouble us and call us to action. The cry to be a 'citizen, no more, no less' has resonated down the ages from the Israelites trapped in Egypt to the migrants imprisoned in Yarl's Wood today. This Lent course has taken the time to examine the issues that arise when states and corporations deny citizens their rights and abuse them. It has asked you to consider as a Christian how you should respond to such situations of injustice. It has asked that you might consider where God is in the suffering and what we 'little people' can do. It has asked you not to walk past like the priest or Levite and to recognise that we are called to be the Good Samaritan, however, hard that might be. As Desmond Tutu, the former Archbishop of Cape Town once said, neutrality for Christians, is not an option:

> 'If you are neutral in situations of injustice, you have chosen the side of the oppressor. If an elephant has its foot on the tail of a mouse and you say that you are neutral, the mouse will not appreciate your neutrality.'
>
> Desmond Tutu

I, Daniel Blake is one man's tragic story in a harsh and unjust world. In the light of our Lenten journey to Jesus' death and resurrection it challenges us to resist oppression, offer compassion, and act in solidarity with those who suffer. For this, in the end, is what Jesus is inviting us to do.

> 'For I was hungry and you gave me something to eat, I was thirsty and you gave me something to drink, I was a stranger and you invited me in. I needed clothes and you clothed me, I was sick and you looked after me, I was in prison and you came to visit me.'
>
> Matt 25:30–35

Although the film focuses on the issue of the work capability assessment, it reminds us that if we want to live in a world where justice prevails human rights are essential for all, not just the privileged few. It reminds us that human rights are precious and need to be protected.

Our current understanding of human rights emerged in 1948 when the newly formed United Nations came together to produce the Declaration of Human Rights.[1] This important document was in response not only to the horrors of the Second World War and the Holocaust, but a century where other human rights abuses on a mass scale had occurred such as Stalin's pogroms and the Armenian Genocide. The preamble declares:

> 'Whereas recognition of the inherent dignity and of the equal and inalienable rights of all members of the human family is the foundation of freedom, justice and peace in the world.
>
> Whereas disregard and contempt for human rights have resulted in barbarous acts which have outraged the conscience of mankind, and the advent of a world in which human beings shall enjoy freedom of speech and belief and freedom from fear and want has been proclaimed as the highest aspiration of the common people.
>
> Whereas it is essential, if man is not to be compelled to have recourse, as a last resort, to rebellion against tyranny and oppression, that

human rights should be protected by the rule of law.

Whereas it is essential to promote the development of friendly relations between nations.

Whereas the peoples of the United Nations have in the Charter reaffirmed their faith in fundamental human rights, in the dignity and worth of the human person and in the equal rights of men and women and have determined to promote social progress and better standards of life in larger freedom.

Whereas Member States have pledged themselves to achieve, in cooperation with the United Nations, the promotion of universal respect for and observance of human rights and fundamental freedoms.

Whereas a common understanding of these rights and freedoms is of the greatest importance for the full realization of this pledge, Now, therefore, The General Assembly, Proclaims this Universal Declaration of Human Rights as a common standard of achievement for all peoples and all nations, to the end that every individual and every organ of society, keeping this Declaration constantly in mind, shall strive by teaching and education to promote respect for these rights and freedoms and by progressive measures, national and international, to secure their universal and effective recognition and observance, both among the peoples of Member States themselves and among the peoples of territories under their jurisdiction.'[2]

It is a powerful statement about equality and justice, and the articles that follow deal with every aspect of human living: beliefs, movement, health, housing, family, law and many more. The fact that at the time of signing, only eight countries abstained, and none dissented, suggests it is one of the best examples of international cooperation of the twentieth century. But as we approach its eightieth anniversary it feels as if the optimism and generosity of spirit that underpinned it have been threatened. There have always been countries who have failed to respect the Declaration resulting in campaign groups like Amnesty International and Human Rights Watch documenting and challenging these. When I was younger it felt as though the majority of human rights abuses happened in countries where there was little democracy. However, since 9/11 the impact of terrorism on Western government has led to increasingly restrictive laws relating to detention of suspects, prison sentences and surveillance.[3] While here in the UK, Brexit has resulted in many on the right calling for an end to the Human Rights Act, with the Prime Minister not ruling out changes after the Manchester bombing and London Bridge attack.[4] And, as we have seen in this Lent course, it is not just terrorist suspects, but sick and disabled people suffering benefits abuses and migrants locked in detention centres who also struggle to achieve full rights in our society. The fact that we have seen such scenes in Britain today, a country which claims to be democratic and fair, means we cannot take human rights for granted. We need to challenge the incursions we have already experienced and be vigilant to ensure we don't lose the rights that we have.

Fighting such battles can feel hard and wearisome. I know I frequently want to give up. And yet, though *I, Daniel Blake* ends in tragedy, it also inspires us not to give up. Injustice can be overcome, and it is.

A recent video by the singer Kesha demonstrates this point beautifully. Over the last few years Kesha has been embroiled in a series of legal battles with her producer Dr Luke, who she alleges abused her, something he denies.[5] Following a recent settlement, she is no longer contracted to work with him, and her single 'Praying' documents her response. The video begins with her in a dream lying in bed while two people with pig's heads stand above her, and then shifts to show her lying on a float in the water, in the position of a crucifix. Her voiceover talks about her despair, questioning whether God exists, whether she can live in a world without hope. When the song begins, we see her walking through her past ripping up the words – symbols of the contract that oppressed her – to create a prayer mound preaching God is love. Her song is a prayer of forgiveness and hope, and the video ends with her rising from her float, and walking on water, to a new beginning.[6] It's a profound and inspiring answer to the situation that she found herself and a brilliant expression of the Resurrection reinterpreted in her own way.

As we come to the end of our Lent course and embark on Holy Week and the events that we know will lead us to the Resurrection, we can reflect on three things. Jesus' witness and suffering has given us a mission always to act for the good of others. We are united in solidarity with fellow campaigners and those who suffer. And when the going gets tough, we look to God for guidance and he answers.

> 'The word of the Lord is faithful
> and all his works to be trusted.
> The Lord loves justice and right
> and fills the earth with his love'.

Psalm 32

NOTES FOR CONCLUSION

1. The Universal Declaration of Human Rights, 1947. http://www.un.org/en/universal-declaration-human-rights/ Ibid.

2. 'The hollowing of human rights in a post 9/11 world', Narjis Khan, Islamic Human Rights Commission, 20th December 2016. http://www.ihrc.org.uk/publications/briefings/11819-the-hollowing-of-human-rights-in-the-post-911-world.

3. 'May: I'll rip up human rights laws that impeded terror legislation', Rowena Mason and Vikram Dodd, *Guardian*, 6th June 2017. https://www.theguardian.com/politics/2017/jun/06/theresa-may-rip-up-human-rights-laws-impede-new-terror-legislation

4. 'Kesha versus Dr Luke', Wikipedia. https://en.wikipedia.org/wiki/Kesha_v._Dr._Luke

5. Kesha, 'Praying', Official video. https://www.youtube.com/watch?v=v-Dur3uXXCQ

ReSOUЯCeS

USEFUL ORGANISATIONS

Policy organisations

Centre for Welfare Reform, www.cforwr.org

Ekklesia, http://www.ekklesia.co.uk/

The Equality Trust, https://www.equalitytrust.org.uk/

The Joint Public Issues Team, http://www.
jointpublicissues.org.uk/

Praxis, http://www.praxis.org.uk/

Refugee Council, https://www.refugeecouncil.org.uk/

Tax Justice Network, http://www.taxjustice.net/

Tax Research UK, http://www.taxresearch.org.uk/
Blog/richard-murphy/

Together for the Common Good, http://www.
togetherforthecommongood.co.uk/

Campaign and support organisations

BlackTriangle, http://blacktrianglecampaign.org/

Catholic Worker Farm, http://www.

londoncatholicworker.org/CWfarm.htm

Campaign Against Arms Trade, https://www.caat.org.uk/

Child Poverty Action Group, http://cpag.org.uk/

Citizen Network, www.citizen-network.org

Disabled People against Cuts, https://dpac.uk.net/

End Hunger Fast, http://www.endhungerfast.co.uk/

Faith and Resistance Network, https://
faithandresistanceblog.wordpress.com/

Joint Council for the Welfare of Immigrants, https://
www.jcwi.org.uk/

London Catholic Worker, http://www.
londoncatholicworker.org/

Migrant Rights Network, http://www.migrantsrights.
org.uk/

Migrant Voice, http://www.migrantvoice.org/

The People's Assembly Against Austerity, http://www.
thepeoplesassembly.org.uk/

Voices for Creative Nonviolence, http://vcnv.org.uk/

Resource Materials

Atos Stories: Monologues and Play about the Basic
income is a just alternative to punitive welfare
systems. Well worth finding out about, http://www.
basicincome.org.uk

Capability Assessment. Downloadable for free from
https://wowpetition.com/atos-stories/

Refugee voices: Refugee stories. http://www.refugee-action.org.uk/refugee-voices/

Child refugees: Stories of child refugees://www.refugee-action.org.uk/refugee-voices/

Homelessness: Real life stories of homeless people. http://www.mungos.org/about/real_life_stories

Hunger: Real stories of people going hungry. https://www.trusselltrust.org/what-we-do/real-stories/

Welfare cuts: Memorial to people who have died due to benefits changes. http://calumslist.org/

Justice and Peace Stations of the Cross: http://www.justice-and-peace.org.uk/resources/stations-of-the-cross/

ACKNOWLEDGEMENTS

I would like to thank David Moloney for inviting me to write this Lent Course. Thanks also to Paul Laverty and Ken Loach for making the film I, Daniel Blake for giving us their blessing and allowing us to use an image from the film for our front cover. Bernadette Meaden and Fran Walsh both gave me very helpful feedback about the content of the course.

I would also like to thank the many activists I have met over the last five years who continue to challenge welfare reform often at great personal cost particularly everyone involved in DPAC, Black Triangle, Pat's Petition and the WOW Petition. Without their courage and witness, which invited me to join the campaign, this book would never have been written.

Thank you too, to everyone at DLT involved in creating and promoting this book: David Moloney, Helen Porter, Virginia Hearn, Judy Linard, Lisa-Jayne Lewis, Will Parkes and Phil Groom.

Finally, I would like to thank my husband Chris, and children Beth, Claire and Jonathan, who have put up with my absences in the evening and at weekends as I've completed this book. I couldn't do it without you.

A donation from the sales of this book will be made to the work of Disabled People Against Cuts and Black Triangle.